THAT PECKHAM BOY

THAT PECKHAM BOY

GROWING UP, GETTING OUT AND GIVING BACK

KENNY IMAFIDON

torva

TRANSWORLD PUBLISHERS
Penguin Random House, One Embassy Gardens,
8 Viaduct Gardens, London sw11 7bw
www.penguin.co.uk

Transworld is part of the Penguin Random House group of companies
whose addresses can be found at global.penguinrandomhouse.com

First published in Great Britain in 2023 by Torva
an imprint of Transworld Publishers

This book is a work of non-fiction based on the life, experiences and recollections
of the author. In some cases names of people, places, dates, sequences and the
detail of events have been changed to protect the privacy of others.

A CIP catalogue record for this book
is available from the British Library.

ISBN 9781911709190

Typeset in 13.5/16 pt Bembo Book MT Pro by Jouve (UK), Milton Keynes.
Printed and bound in Great Britain by Clays Ltd, Elcograf S.p.A.

The authorized representative in the EEA is Penguin Random House Ireland,
Morrison Chambers, 32 Nassau Street, Dublin D02 YH68.

Penguin Random House is committed to a sustainable future
for our business, our readers and our planet. This book is made
from Forest Stewardship Council® certified paper.

Dedicated to all those who seek hope and to those who need reminding: you are much more than the worst thing you've ever done. Our past does not define us, only our daily actions matter from now on.

Contents

1

Daddy Issues

*'My generation is the most fatherless and insecure
generation that's ever lived, and we are willing to
sacrifice everything if we just can be told we are loved.
If only we knew just how loved we really are.'*
– Jefferson Bethke, *Jesus > Religion*

'Open the door!'

I couldn't see her, but I knew she was standing on the other side of the door. Arms crossed. Frowning. I flapped at the stiff letter box, crouching down to shout through it.

'Open the door, then!' I tried again.

I was thirteen years old, and it was late – well past my curfew and well past my bedtime. I was in the wrong, I knew this, but I was home now, wasn't I? Mum could cut me some slack.

In my just-a-size-too-big of an adidas tracksuit,

I could feel the cold winter breeze grazing the back of my neck and I shivered.

'Just let me inside,' I shouted, this time at the top of my lungs, desperation lingering in the edges of my voice. From the other side of the door, my mother finally hollered back.

'Go back to where you came from!' she shouted. Now I knew for sure she was there. I kept flapping the letter box with no concern for the neighbours that I woke up that night. They were used to it. Me and my brother George were the only kids living in the small close of six houses, and this wasn't the first time I'd been locked out by her. I looked around. The branches on the only tree in a central patch of grass opposite twisted upwards towards the dark sky.

'I can't. Please let me in,' I yelled. Eventually, she'd start to feel sorry for me, I figured. Or at least, she'd want me to stop making all this noise for the neighbours' sake. She cared about them far more than I did. She wouldn't want a scene. All I was determined to do was make this woman let me in.

I tried shouting a few times more, and banging the letter box, but Mum did not budge. You would have thought she had noise-cancelling headphones on the way she pretended she couldn't hear. Maybe, after so many years, she was as good at tuning out the commotion around her as I was. It had gone on too long now, and one of us had to give in. I let go of the letter box, letting it clatter shut one last time, and resigned myself to the night.

Now I had to consider what my mum had told me earlier: 'Go back to where you came from.' Leaning up against the fence in the unlit pathway, I explored my options. Where could I go? Adam's house? Or Sam's house maybe? I had plenty of friends near by. I'd just come from Sam's anyway – a ten minute cycle from where I lived. I had thought to leave earlier, but lost track of time. We were studying, but we got sidetracked into a hilarious group call with other friends, we were all bantering each other and crying tears of laughter. Anyway, I wasn't laughing now, and this felt like a trick – I knew that if I actually did what she said, if I actually went back to where I'd come from, I could be in even more trouble. For a split second, another thought crossed my mind. Should I just boot down the door? Was I strong enough? But then reality slapped me in the face: I'd get an even worse booting back if I did that, and with my skinny frame it would be impossible anyway. I was stuck. There was no way out of this one.

I trudged back up to the door.

'Open the door, *please*. I'm *sorryyyyy*,' I whined, desperate to get inside to the light, to the warmth. But that night my mum was hell-bent on not just teaching me a lesson, but making sure I felt it too.

From the letter box I saw her turn and disappear into the living room. Now, the flicker from the TV was visible through the sliver in the door. I pictured her on the sofa, arms folded watching her Nollywood film – the low-budget films she loved to watch from Nigeria – just waiting until I'd given up all hope. My mum was warm, caring and loving. But she was also not a pushover. She was a real disciplinarian. She played no games.

So there I was, stuck outside on a cold night in London. Peckham to be precise. Not long ago it was voted as the 'coolest neighbourhood to live in in the UK' by *Time Out* – two years in a row, even. These days estate agents use words like 'fun' and 'quirky' to describe it. Yuppies drink pink and orange cocktails from bars on top of buildings. But on the streets, that wasn't the Peckham I grew up in. In my Peckham, kids from the estates played football with makeshift goalposts. The sellers on Rye Lane offered everything from cheap cuts of meat to second-hand mobile phones, with replica chargers. The lane was filled with pound stores, and stalls selling you three plantains for a pound. Barbershops and hair salons were parked on each corner and the fishmongers dumped their ice on the pavement at the end of the day's shift. In the streets I grew up in, Peckham Boys operated in both plain sight and in the shadows. Now, they are discreet cogs making sure the drugs machine keeps

turning and the arts students and 'young professionals' in the flats above get their supply. In my
Peckham, police sirens were heard daily, like a top-
ten song you'd hear on the radio. Violence hung in
the air like a bad smell.

Once inside my home, I was living in Benin
City, Nigeria. Whatever laws protected me as a
child in the UK had no jurisdiction within these
walls. It was another country, another culture.
And I knew the consequences. I knew that when
I breached curfew – and I did, often – I would be
locked out on London's cold streets. There were
times when I truly had no other option but to
return to my friends' houses, no matter what time
of day, and seek refuge.

But today I was lucky. Later, and only God
knows how long later, I heard the rattle of chains
being removed and the creak of the door hinge as
it opened. Finally, my mum had found it in her
heart to let me in.

I rushed inside, just in case she thought about
changing her mind, but I wasn't free yet. She
blocked the way, standing between me and the
stairs, chest puffed out with a deep frown etched
on her brow. Then, she leaned in and sniffed at the
air around me. I knew what it was. I stunk of mari-
juana. I hadn't smoked it myself – while I'd been at
Sam's, we'd briefly gone to chat to some friends on
the top floor stairwell in his block of flats. No one

would dare smoke a spliff in their parents' home, so they found quiet places and dark corners to hide in. But the smell had stuck to my clothes, and nothing got past my mum.

'I hope you are not taking any drugs?'

The question was rhetorical. If she really thought I was smoking weed, I would have felt her belt across the palms of my hands long before I heard about what I had done wrong, or supposedly done wrong. Or she'd make me kneel and face the wall for what felt like an eternity.

'I don't smoke and never have, you know this; it was other people,' I replied, trying to edge past her to run upstairs.

'Kenny, you need to be careful and not hang around with the wrong crowd,' my mum continued. 'Because . . .'

I'd heard this all before. The rest of what she was saying was just noise, and I had already tuned out. My mum could leave her words of wisdom to herself. I just wanted to be in my safe space, the first room on the left at the top of the stairs. The room where I could shut the door and be away from everything – kind of.

Aged thirteen, I shared a room with my little brother, George. Later, Mum would give him her room and she would sleep on the sofa downstairs, but for now we had one double bed to share. With almost four years between us, George looked up to me and wanted to follow my every move. I was a curious, confident teenager desperate to get out from Mum's clutches and find my way in the world, drawn in by my peer group and wanting to fit in. George picked up on my new-found sense of freedom and always pleaded with me to bring him along, but I never did. What teenage boy wants his little brother around to take care of? But when it came to Mum we had an unspoken pact. If one of us was in trouble – perhaps someone had stolen extra food from the kitchen, that Mum had carefully rationed – then we kept our mouths shut. 'I don't know anything,' he'd shrug if Mum ever asked, and I would do the same. He was often awake, waiting up for me when I came home late after curfew.

My room was also packed full of Mum's clutter. We lived in a small, rented, two-bedroom house, which was overcrowded then and still is now with the hoarded items that my mother swears will be going back to Nigeria someday. Clothes, shoes, documents – suitcases packed with these covered every inch of every room and spilled into mine, my safe space. I had no posters on the stark white walls, just a big wardrobe sat against one wall with four wide doors, half of it packed full of more of my mum's blouses and dresses and jackets, with more suitcases piled on top. The only items that made that room my own were the television and

PlayStation that I used to play with George: *GTA Vice City*, *The Urbz: Sims in the City* and *Pro Evolution Soccer 5* cases stacked neatly next to it. That night, I slipped under the duvet next to him, breathed a long deep breath and finally closed my eyes.

I was born in King's College Hospital in south-east London in May 1993, and my birth certificate has just my mother's name on it. Mum blessed me in an un-Nigerian way with just three names, as opposed to the traditional seven or eight names Nigerian newborns are usually given. Kenny Izingbeuwa (pronounced e-zeh-boo-wa) Imafidon. I share my full name boldly now, I own it — although growing up in south-east London I wasn't always so proud of my African-sounding middle name.

My powerful and purposeful names, like so many other African names, didn't roll off the tongue for everybody. To avoid being mocked in school for having a name that was difficult to spell and tricky to pronounce, I kept it to myself. My White classmates had 'easy-to-say' names, familiar names, names they didn't even know the meaning or origin of. But names are important. How many people know a Charles who understands that their name means 'free man'? My middle name means 'patience in wealth'.

My mother, Dorah Eseosa Onaghise, was a

Nigerian Queen who gave birth to me at thirty-seven years old. She took pride in how she dressed but never cared to wear make-up. Instead, she radiated beauty from her face that was ever-fresh and line-free, despite her stress. Less than a year before I came along, she had left everything she knew – the life she had built for herself over 3,000 miles away in Benin City, Edo State, Nigeria – to settle in London. All in the selfless pursuit of giving us a better start in life. But she had traded in her comfortable, sweet life in Nigeria for a life of poverty, debt and high blood pressure in England.

When she first moved here, the internet wasn't widely available. There was no such thing as Zoom, FaceTime or WhatsApp. Hard to imagine it now. Instead, she would buy £5 international calling cards just to talk to family back home. I remember this vividly, as when I was old enough I was the unlucky person who got sent to the shop on a weekly basis to buy them. Without those cards she was isolated.

And like so many immigrants before her, I also remember the days she spent working long hours for low wages and little stability, juggling multiple cleaning jobs to keep a roof over our heads, food in our fridge and clothes on our backs. My brother and I would see her in the morning before she left for work, and then at home after school, before she put on her shoes again and returned to another job in the evening. Every day my mum did this.

With Mum living from pay cheque to pay cheque and working tirelessly, it was a given that state benefits were not an option in our house. Though from where I was standing, a teenage boy who saw and understood how hard her life was, I felt she needed it. She could have done with the extra support, but the Nigerian spirit in her was strong and she was adamant that we wouldn't rely on government handouts. She had too much pride. Besides, it was not just my brother and I who were financially dependent on my mother, but also the family she had left behind.

'I'll try my best to send you the money next week.' These were words I often heard Mum say over the phone to extended family. Other people might say that and not actually mean it, but my mum always meant it. As she sat on the sofa with the phone to her ear, I could almost see the calculator in her mind doing the sums: how very little plus very little could all add up to something that she could wire across. And Mum never let people down.

While my family in London was tiny, in Nigeria it was far from it. My dad has nine boys (including me) and six girls, from four different marriages. Before I was born, my mum had three girls and one boy from a previous partner who she was traditionally married to. Between them, that's a lot of children. In total that makes one full brother – that's George – and eighteen half-brothers and sisters. The way I like to look at it, it's a starting eleven for a football team plus a decent roster of subs.

Even though Mum was earning a shoestring of a salary, she was a philanthropist without the high net worth. Maybe it was because in Nigeria she had witnessed poverty unlike anything I had ever seen. What passed for poverty here was luxury for someone there, so she accepted it. But she also had a heart that wanted to give, and was generous to a fault. She would go above and beyond for others, including strangers, people she barely knew. Before she gave up her own bedroom full-time for George, there were times when she would give it up (or, annoyingly, give up my room) to visitors when they stayed over. Irritated and uncomfortable with the intrusion, I would think to myself: why would you willingly sleep on the couch, while a guest who should simply be grateful for a roof over their head sleeps in your bed? That could never be me.

So, my mother was rich in spirit but poor in pounds, but try telling this to our family in Nigeria who relied on her for everything: money for school fees or for clothing and food. These were people who had never left their country and so they imagined that England's streets were paved in gold, that all we had to do in the capital to earn good money was to breathe it in. They had no clue how expensive it is to live here, or how badly paid so many jobs are. They couldn't comprehend that the little money Mum received in one hand, was very quickly taken away from the other through bills, taxes and other expenses like childcare and travel.

But my mother would never dream of telling them the truth or complaining. During all those phone calls, I never once heard her say: 'Sorry, there isn't enough to go around.' She would rather take on suffering herself than see them suffer. As I would watch her, quietly watching her films after her long working days, often the first sit-down she would have had in 12 hours, I would think: who is your financial sponsor? Who will pay off your debts?

This is life for so many immigrants. The responsibilities are real, and Mum accepted hers. No matter how tough life got personally, she never faulted on her commitments – to me or George or her family back home.

'Kenny, are you going to tell me where you were?' Mum questioned me. Even by the next morning she hadn't let go of what happened the night before, and why I was so late home.

'Sam's place. Using his computer,' I mumbled

while keeping my head down, trying to eat my breakfast.

'So, you couldn't look at your watch and leave on time?'

'We were studying, Mum. I always go to Sam's to study. You know that,' I replied, trying to fend her off.

It wasn't a lie. Although the internet was now everywhere, my family was on the wrong side of the digital divide. I never had a laptop or a computer at home because my mum simply couldn't afford to buy me one. If I ever had to do homework that needed research and a computer, I would have to go to an internet café or Sam's home to use his. He didn't mind. But I did. Of course, I would have loved it if my dad had stepped up and offered to buy me one, but that would probably never happen.

Much like 2.9 million other children growing up in the UK today, I grew up in a single parent home.[1] And like almost one in five children, I grew up without a father in the picture.[2] When it came to my dad, well, me and him were as close as London is to Dubai – not close at all. And even that's an understatement. I never heard the words 'Happy birthday, son,' leave his mouth. I never read the words written in a birthday card or in a text message either. I'm convinced he didn't know when my birthday was, but I did remember his – if that counts for something.

I could never decide whether he was a man of few words, or whether it was just me he didn't have much to say to. We never spoke about what it means to be a man, or how to have a healthy relationship with a girl. I would have loved to have told him about my first crush, but he wasn't there to talk to. He wasn't on the touchline at any of my football games, cheering me on alongside other parents. We never visited the park together. He wasn't around to teach me how to ride my first bicycle, either. There were no words of affirmation or encouragement. The conversations we had were mostly short and emotionless. After a while, what was there to say?

Any time we did spend together was mostly forgettable. So I've forgotten. I don't even remember being hugged by him. When we did meet, we would shake hands like colleagues at a business meeting. As if that was the only kind of relationship he knew and understood how to do well.

My dad was a highly successful businessman. Like Mum, he'd come from humble beginnings, growing up in a small village in the same state in Nigeria as her. He had made it from rags to riches – literally – and knew first-hand what poverty looked and felt like. Because of this money and success, people seemed to worship the ground he walked on. In the culture we are from, money talks and it talks loudly. Ultimately, it's the thing that determines your social standing and the respect you command. Respectfully, being father-of-the-year in a British sense – taking your son to football practice or on bike rides – is nothing more than a nice-to-have in Nigerian culture. It's all about the money, and you either have it or, as my Naija people say, 'If you no get money, hide your face.' Translation: if you are broke, keep quiet, mind your business and stay in your corner.

He extended this businessman mentality into the way he treated me. As I say, birthday cards were out of the question, but whenever he saw me, he'd pull out a crisp stack of flamingo-pink £50 notes totalling maybe two or three hundred pounds, sometimes more, and hand it to me. I like to think that this was his love language, his way of showing that he did care about the son whose birthday he wouldn't have been able to tell you. Being a kid and receiving this golden money was the highlight of every one of his visits – it was rare, seeing stacks of cash bundled up together in one large amount, treasure to take home and hide in secret corners of my room. As much as I disliked him, disliked all the gaps he'd left in my upbringing, I didn't dislike free money. Who does? So I swallowed my pride, and I took it gladly.

The problem was that he only saw me a few times a year, when he came to visit London. At home, I saw just how little this money actually helped. A couple of hundred pounds a couple of times a year was nothing in comparison to how much my mum spent on us day in, day out, just to keep us alive. Conscious about the cost of living, I knew that I couldn't keep this money for myself and I needed to help out too. But it didn't make sense. I didn't want lump sums from my dad. I wanted his financial support consistently. Why was it left to my mum to carry the burden, particularly when he had the broader shoulders – and the businessman bank account – to take on more? And of course, when it came down to it I wanted him to care about the position I was in and get me out of it. But even more than money, I wanted his love.

My dad should have been my first male role model, but he wasn't. I knew from early on that despite not having the slightest idea of what type of man I wanted to be in the future, I unquestionably didn't want to be anything like him. I had to – no, I *needed* to – do and be better than him. Education, I thought, was the best way to do that. I was a sharp kid, even as a youngster. I picked up subjects quickly, excelled in sports, and my grades were always good. Despite how much I enjoyed playing out, I always made sure my homework was done, scribbling through it quickly so that I could go kick a ball outside before my curfew kicked in. And despite me breaking those curfews, deep down Mum knew I wasn't a bad kid. Mostly, she just got tired of me coming home late from Sam's with the same excuse. She could see I was bright, and I think it bothered her that she could never give me the tools, like a computer, to study at home.

Not long after my performance outside the front door, she encouraged me to write a letter to my dad. 'Ask him to buy you the laptop. Explain that you need it for your studies,' she instructed. He could afford it, after all. I was hesitant at first. *Why do I need to write this guy a whole damn letter just to get a laptop? Is this what other kids have to do?* The guy was my dad, not some member of a jury I needed to sway. Should I really have to put together a convincing case for him? But my mum was sure that if I explained very clearly how my studies were being negatively impacted by the absence of a laptop, my dad would get me one. It was the sort of argument that should appeal to a Nigerian parent who is a firm believer in education and academic excellence, she said.

I wrote it reluctantly, hunched over the table in the overcrowded living room where my mum spent most of her non-working hours, sitting in the permanent dip she'd created over the years in her favourite spot on the sofa. I struggled to find the words to write as she watched her Nollywood movie next to me. I gripped the pen hard. It wasn't until the credits began to roll that I finally finished it.

Mum sent it on to my dad in Nigeria. And then I waited. I tried to do the maths in my head: how long does it take for a letter to arrive overseas? How much time would it take for a reply to come back, on average? But the days turned to weeks and the weeks turned to months. I never got a response, let alone a laptop. When I finally realized, after months of waiting, that no answer was coming, I was surprised at my own surprise. This was my dad for you. After that the only feelings I had for him were of bitterness and resentment. How could he not even acknowledge me? How could he not respond to such a heartfelt letter?

Of course, my mum could have reeled off ninety-nine reasons to justify my feelings, but she kept them to herself. She was better than most. She never turned me against him or tried to use me as a weapon to punish him. Mostly, I overheard things, spoken to friends in her close-knit circle. 'That man does not support me,' she'd complain in her private, but at times opera-loud, voice. But there wasn't an idealized image of my dad to ruin. He had already single-handedly done all the work of diminishing himself. In my eyes, he had abandoned us. We were out of sight and out of mind. But it was a lot for a kid to figure out, and I spent a lot of time going over it in my mind. I kept asking: why

was I suffering so much more than I had to? But
the answer was always the same: it was because of
him. I was living in poverty – a poverty that he
knew and had lived through himself. Why did he
want us to live as he'd lived? Why didn't he want
better for us?

I probably would have understood if the reason
was as simple as Mum and Dad not getting along.
Relationships fail. I could see that all around me.
So many of my friends lived with only one
parent – if anything, you stood out if both parents
lived happily together. Now that was unusual. I
could have looked past that reality if he'd looked
after us. But I couldn't look past the fact that my
circumstances seemed to be a result of collateral
damage beyond my control. This wasn't just a
failed relationship. It was a relationship devoid of
any co-parenting. No shared responsibility. And,
from my father, no love.

From what I understood of the world, kids with
rich fathers like mine attended private schools – at the
very least they were sent to the best state schools in
good catchment areas. I'd wonder about their spa-
cious and beautiful homes and those annual family
trips. I'd seen the TV shows, the adverts full of
smiling holiday faces, the evidence of how it was
meant to be. Never had I seen a living room ceiling
like ours, left wide open in an angry yawn for a
year and a half because of flooding from the

upstairs bathroom. Never had I seen mould growing on the walls.

Young as I was, I could see that my dad was
shockingly stingy, astonishingly absent, and un-
believably unempathetic. And all those people
who considered my father to be the money man,
the big *oga* at the top, never seemed to include in
their judgement of his character his ability to be a
good father. In my opinion, he was the perfect
example of a public success story but a private failure. Society — both British and Nigerian, and
plenty of others too — celebrate fathers who are
merely present in their kids' lives. This is like clapping a fish for swimming. We don't praise mothers
for simply being present in their children's lives,
because it's a given.

I am not a dad, but I do know that fatherhood
isn't easy. I'm in no position to judge what is and
isn't possible. But I can comment as someone who
has grown up with an absent dad, who I felt never
loved me. That is my truth. I am sure my dad had
his reasons, but I was a child and could not possibly
understand those decisions. I just wanted him to be
present. I just wanted to be hugged. I just wanted
to be heard.

Now I know it's affected me in more ways
than I can comprehend. I've since read studies that
show how having a father like mine affects a child's
social and emotional development.[3] We may have

difficulty with self-control, talking about our feelings, or asking for help. We may have difficulty showing affection to others. Aggression, violence, lawbreaking and vandalism are more likely in children like us.[4] I've read that the effects may be worse if a father disappears during early childhood. Some say it's worse for boys than for girls.[5]

As a boy and as a young man, I displayed many of the symptoms of a fatherless kid. I was angry, unwilling and unable to express my feelings. I hate to say it, but I had daddy issues. And possibly still have. The truth is, I was a true mummy's boy, but not entirely because I wanted to be – I didn't have the choice. My mum loved me, she was proud of me and I knew it. But she was also the one who had to discipline me, the one who had to lock the door when I stayed out past curfew, the one who had to raise me alone. She tried as hard as she could to fill that gap that she couldn't quite squeeze into, so I did what many kids in my position do. I found my male role models elsewhere: I turned my attention to the streets.

2

My Brother's Keeper

'I believe in the brotherhood of all men, but I don't believe in wasting brotherhood on anyone who doesn't want to practise it with me. Brotherhood is a two-way street.' – Malcolm X

Who do you look up to? Some people are admired because they've achieved something extraordinary, against all odds. Others are admired because of their wealth or the position they have risen to. Some may hold a world record or are extremely gifted and have had those talents nurtured. Others may have tirelessly campaigned for social change – maybe even given their lives so that we can enjoy the freedoms we have today.

Every October when Black History Month rolled around, our history teachers would fill us with stories of civil rights marches and momentous speeches, like Dr Martin Luther King Jr's famous 'I Have a Dream' speech. The three towering figures of the American civil rights movement, Dr Martin Luther King Jr, Malcolm X, and Marcus Garvey, entered my consciousness in the classroom and left a strong impression of what inspirational leader-ship looks like, a blueprint I could follow to become the great man my father never was. I wanted to be like them. I wanted to command respect like them.

But greatness looked a little different closer to home. I admired figures who I saw every day around the concrete tower blocks that filled the Peckham skyline. These guys were also influential, respected and successful; leaders in their own right, whose confidence and conviction also drew people to them. These guys were drug dealers. And I wanted to be like them, too.

I remember the day I first met my first role model. I was a kid, still in primary school, playing football with a few friends in a makeshift football cage in the estate opposite home. We called it the pit. It was surrounded by concrete, so if you fell down hard enough you would be aching at best and, at worst, left with an open wound. It gave an edge to the game, raised the stakes somehow. Femi was older than me by ten years or so, watching us from the side of the pit, smirking because he knew he could run rings around the rest of us. When the urge to prove this took over, he jumped in and showed us what he was about. He took pleasure in it too.

Femi wasn't bothered that we were kids. When he got in the pit, we were his audience. Femi had skills, our own Cristiano Ronaldo, showing off his footwork just because he could. He was wiping the floor with us for fun. He'd nutmeg one boy called Lorenzo, casually clipping the ball with his toe and passing it through his legs – a humiliation hard to live down. And no matter how hard we tried we couldn't wrestle the ball off him. But his Achilles heel was that he had the stamina of a hippo. The brother could play for ten minutes, tops – it must have been all that weed he was smoking – and he tapped out of the game as quickly as he had tapped in. Yet I was in awe of him, imagining a day when I would be as big and have football skills like him too.

'Good game,' I nodded as he caught his breath on the sidelines, his hands resting on his knees.

In return, he offered some advice on my own technique, and we continued chatting. It turned out we didn't live so far from each other, and from that day on, as I grew up around the area, he remembered my face. When we passed each other in the street, we'd nod to each other or fist-bump. When we exchanged numbers, that felt even better. Because Femi was older, it felt as though he was taking me under his wing.

Through Femi I met Dwayne. Both were in

their twenties, Femi a little younger, and both had been to prison by the time I began hanging around them. They were the total opposites; Femi was tall, dark-skinned and fairly chubby, and Dwayne was a short guy with long plaited hair and a lighter complexion. They were inseparable, like patty and bread. It was a kind of closeness I envied and wanted to be a part of. They were always joking around with each other, and would easily give each other money if one needed it, even sharing cars. As far as I could see, they had it all: money, power, respect, and countless women who wanted to be around them. 'Gotta go, bruv. I'm linking one ting,' they'd say before driving to Hackney or Camden or wherever a girlfriend lived. Or I'd see girls chilling in the back seats of their cars, tinted windows wound down. Compared to me, they seemed like rock stars with expensive cars, designer clothes and lavish homes. It was a lifestyle I wanted to grab hold of and not let go.

As they got used to me, it became normal to hang around them. They might send me to the corner shop to get food, and let me keep the change, a simple favour. As I got older, they let me be a part of their circle, chilling with them properly in their homes, talking and playing computer games while they smoked weed. Male role models were thin on the ground and these guys were as good as it got.

My interest in them was reciprocated, and over

time they became like surrogate big brothers. They wanted the best for me, genuinely – which was much more than I could say for my own father. But as much as she disapproved of him, my mum would not have approved of Femi and Dwayne as role models and mentors either. She would not have seen them as people to look up to, these big boys in their big cars, and she would not see the good in them that I could see.

Yet strangely, all of their ambitions for me were mostly aligned. Like Mum, Dwayne and Femi wanted me to grow and end up in the right rooms, sitting in a lecture hall at an elite university, not in a prison cell like them. 'You want to get out of the hood, Kenny? Take your studies seriously. Work hard and get the grades,' they often told me, perhaps because they knew if I didn't I'd be stuck there, like them. Truthfully, they might have looked like 'bad guys', but they wanted me to be all right. And their actions spoke louder than words: they would slip me some money on occasion, or drop me off at a friend's house if I needed a lift. My mum had no clue that in the hood these guys were my guardian angels.

But Dwayne and Femi lived a life of crime. Together, they knew the drug game inside out. Absorbing their world meant absorbing that lifestyle too, watching how they operated, understanding the risks and the rewards. Knowing what door they had opened up and allowed me to peek through, they also felt they had a duty to protect me, to show me how to survive. Having brought me into the jungle, it would have been negligent of them not to pass on a few essential lessons to navigate it. Just for insurance. Just in case.

Lesson one: be on your guard at all times. You can't afford to be someone else's prey. In this jungle, violence is the currency. To be clear, I'd never actually seen Dwayne or Femi commit any proper violence, but I knew that if boys like them got respect, it's because they were feared as well as admired. 'If you have something someone else wants, be it jewellery, money, or that same respect, an invisible target is painted on your back,' they told me. It takes very little to become a victim of armed robbery, grievous bodily harm, or even murder on Peckham's streets. Be alert and willing to do whatever it takes to defend yourself. Better to be judged by twelve in a courtroom than carried by six at your funeral.

Lesson two: keep your circle tight. You can't trust everyone. The snakes are everywhere in the jungle. Sometimes they come in the form of so-called friends. Keep how much money you're making under wraps. Don't let people know where you stash your drugs or money. The people you least expect will be the same people to rob you for all you have.

Lesson three: don't shit where you sleep. This

means do not leave anything that could put you in jail in your own house. Where you rest your head at night needs to be your safe haven and not a storage place for drugs, weapons, or large amounts of money that you can't account for. Leave any of that stuff with a girl you trust or get someone, most likely younger, to store it for you. You may have to pay them, but it isn't always necessary. From semi-automatic machine guns to mountains of cash, only the Lord knows how many homes in Peckham have incriminating items hiding behind family photos and inside couch covers. Call it community spirit.

Because here's the thing: whatever you might think of guys who make their living from dealing drugs, Femi and Dwayne were genuinely kind-hearted guys, who looked out for me. Though they smoked weed habitually, they would have knocked me out if they caught me rolling my own spliff. The same guys that could have exploited me and played on my desire for their approval, in a trade where this happens all too easily to young boys, instead showed me genuine love. It was like the love you have for a little brother. Like the love I had for George. And they accepted me for who I was.

Did being around them corrupt me? Possibly so. But I didn't care. They both had my back, because life in Peckham was unpredictable and you just never knew what to expect.

One incident sticks in my mind. One sunny afternoon, I went to meet with some friends in one of the north Peckham estates, less than a mile from home. I took off on my Specialized bike, a brand which was the Porsche of bicycles at the time. It was fairly new, a gift from Femi and Dwayne, so riding it still felt special. When I arrived, an older guy from the area was hanging around. Devon. He was a few school years above me, with short hair and hands too big for his wrists. He wasn't a friend. Spying my bike he gave it a lookover, then nodded.

'Let me borrow your bike quickly.'

This was the hood; if someone you don't know − or at least don't trust − asks to 'borrow your bike quickly', then two things spring to mind. Firstly, you know for sure it won't be quick, and secondly, they might 'borrow' it, but they definitely won't be bringing it back.

'Nah, bro,' I said firmly, taking all my nerves to keep steady eye contact with him. I watched Devon's eyes squint back at me, but a split second after the words left my mouth I felt a pain throbbing through my skull. I was stumbling backwards, struggling to stay upright.

He had punched me straight in the face.

Now, I could fight if necessary. But looking at this guy in front of me, bigger and stronger and with years of experience on me, I knew I couldn't win. Behind him was also an assortment of other threatening characters from the estate, whose reputations preceded them, and when I did the maths quickly, the numbers didn't add up. There was no way I was going to let them all jump on me or, worse, try to stab me. I knew some of them carried knives. Instead, I gathered my busted-lip self together and cycled off, legs working double time. The heftiness of the hit and the sheer humiliation had left me feeling hot, and I raged with the embarrassment of the whole episode.

A wiser me might have let this incident slide. After all, I still had my bike, didn't I? But to a fourteen-year-old Kenny, revenge tasted a whole lot better than wisdom, and a hell of a lot better than a punch in the face. So, just as any young boy in any other playground across the country might do when attacked by an older boy, I went running to my big brothers.

'Bro, I've just got into a madness and these man try steal my bike!' I shouted down the phone to Dwayne. I told him everything, talking so fast that each word tripped over the next. He listened patiently as I got more worked up about what I was going to do. 'Come. Meet me. We have to circle back there,' I told him. I didn't need to ask twice. He and Femi would be there soon.

Not long after, we returned to the scene of the crime. For Dwayne and Femi this was business as usual, nothing unique about the day. But I was newer to this game and felt there was something oddly satisfying about seeing a bully get bullied by a bigger bully. And I had unfinished business with mine. We searched all the Peckham streets where we thought we might find Devon, to make sure I got nothing short of revenge. Beneath the anger, beneath the throb of where the punch had landed, I was looking forward to the fight.

But there was something wrong. In the park where I expected him to be, Devon was nowhere. And his crazy accomplices from earlier had disappeared too. The air was still. The estate felt quiet. We were exposed, out in the open.

'Oi!'

Suddenly someone shouted behind me, but before I could react, a group of masked men jumped out. We had no clue who they were, and they didn't look like Devon and his mates, either. My heart leapt, and I saw the shock on Dwayne and Femi's faces too. These men were unrecognizable, covered up in hoods and ballies, but waving long, glinting butcher's knives. Those I couldn't miss.

In that split second, we weighed up our options. Pride told us to stay and stand our ground, but pride could also get us killed or on a bed in an intensive care unit. We knew better than to run towards them with our bare fists, so we used our common sense. For the second time that day, I was running away from the scene. They chased us, waving their sharp blades. We scrambled in different directions to break up the pack, knowing these guys were looking to wet their knives with blood.

I was in Usain Bolt mode, thundering through the backstreets. These *Freddy vs. Jason* lookalikes were not going to catch me, no way. But this was no horror movie. This was real life. This was *my* life. I was in grave danger.

We'd come out to hunt, but now we were being hunted. And, unlike us, these guys had found what they were looking for: Peckham Boys. So I kept running until I reached somewhere that felt safe, somewhere closer to home.

By this time the sun had set, and the only lights I could see were from the pale yellow street lights and passing cars. I didn't stop running for a good five minutes, until I could no longer see their masked faces when I turned my head. My legs ached with tiredness but the adrenaline kept me going. Gasping for breath and dehydrated, I eventually found refuge in Clifton Estate. As I slumped down on the concrete steps of a housing block, I could feel my chapped lips. My chest was rising and falling as I gulped in the night air. I desperately needed water, and to shake off the fear of what had just happened. More importantly, I needed to know what happened to Dwayne and Femi. Did they get away, or did they get caught?

Gripped by anxiety, I hesitated before calling Dwayne's mobile.

'Yo.' I latched on to his voice immediately and exhaled with relief. He would have no idea how happy I was to hear him, like a mother who hadn't heard from her loving son in a long while. But before I could hold on to that upbeat feeling, my heart plummeted.

'Femi got caught,' he said urgently. In quick bursts he told me what I needed to know. They'd split up. The gang had followed Femi. They had stabbed him several times in the back and elsewhere on his upper body. An ambulance was coming to get him. Before I could ask any more questions, Dwayne said he had to go. We couldn't talk any more than that on the phone.

When it came to our mobiles, you never knew if the police were listening. We were paranoid, yes. But it was better to be safe than sorry. We didn't want any evidence that could make us look guilty. But guilt overcame me nonetheless. I hated myself for what had happened to Femi. This was all my fault. Nothing would have happened to him if it hadn't been for me bringing him out to teach Devon a lesson. How could I forgive myself if Femi blamed me for it? While he was in the hospital, doctors working hard to patch him up, I couldn't even speak to him. I couldn't check how he was doing or how he was feeling. Might he die? Might he be paralysed? I pictured him lying there drifting in and out of consciousness or cussing me for everything.

A couple of days after the incident, I finally got hold of him. I was by myself, pacing up and down outside my house, just pacing to relieve the tension. After a pause, he answered, but surprisingly there wasn't a hostile tone in his voice. I felt my shoulders soften and the tension lift.

'Bro, it was not your fault. I came with you. You know how it goes. This is the streets, things happen. But I'm glad you're good, though,' he said, reassuringly.

'But you got stabbed!'

'That ain't your fault. It was just wrong place wrong time,' he said, so casually. If it were me, I'd be furious, I thought. And I continued to feel very differently about what happened. But even in the weeks after, Femi treated me no differently and showed me the same love he always had. Like the big brother he was, his actions told me more than any words: he would rather it had happened to him than to me.

I was thankful to God that Femi was still alive and would be able to recover quickly. He was a tough guy, physically and mentally. When the police visited him in hospital for questioning, he told them nothing. See no evil, speak no evil: that was his motto and he refused to elaborate on the incident. Doing so would be against his moral code. And while I was thankful he didn't blame me, my anger over the incident still burned strong. I knew for certain that I couldn't carry on as before.

I knew that, whether I wanted to or not, we had to get these guys back – if we ever found out who they were. No question about it. In the hood, despite how many of us came from religious families, crosses hanging with pride on the backs of bedroom doors, we knew nothing about turning the other cheek and showing others grace. That would be weak. That wasn't our gospel. We were more Old Testament: an eye for an eye, a tooth for a tooth, and to hell with the consequences.

Now, I know what you're thinking. Why didn't we just reach out to the police? The answer is simple: it was never an option for us. *Especially* if we wanted justice. For us, the police weren't a resource for resolving conflict. And truthfully, they still aren't. When they came, if they came at all, we had no trust in them. The Metropolitan Police had a long history of racism and we were always wary. Also, if you helped them in their investigations you'd face being labelled as a 'snitch', and where I'm from this is a suicidal move. A death wish. This code of silence is what keeps so many people in communities like mine in prison, tucked away doing long sentences for crimes they didn't commit, sitting alone in a two-by-three-metre cell knowing full well who did it. Better to spend time in prison than to be a snitch on the outside. That's not a life worth living: you would be in constant fear of attack, but worse than that you would be ostracized by everyone. Just like animals that are branded with a hot iron, you would wear the mark of 'snitch' on your forehead for life.

An old friend, Kwame, is a perfect example of those who refuse to snitch. Now in his late thirties, married with children, he's serving a minimum of thirty years in prison. And all it would have taken was thirty seconds of honesty when he was arrested to give him his freedom. But Femi's code and Kwame's code, it was all the same. Kwame wouldn't snitch. It was death before dishonour, he even has it tattooed on his right arm to prove it.

All he has to live for now is the off-chance his street name is mentioned in a song by one of the rappers from our area, because Kwame made the ultimate sacrifice. As far as the streets are concerned, he 'kept it real'. He stuck to the code. He kept his mouth shut despite whatever it would cost him – his future, his family, his freedom. Perhaps it sounds crazy but one thing's for sure: if I was in his shoes, I would have done the same. I wouldn't have been able to see another way out.

★

So, welcome to Peckham. Just like the rest of the United Kingdom, the streets have their own unwritten constitution. If you grew up in the hood, you felt compelled to pledge allegiance to its codes and live by its rules. It didn't matter whether you were involved in the street life or part of any gangs. You know the saying: 'When in Rome'? Well, when in Peckham, do as the Peckham Boys do. If you didn't, then it would be an understatement to say you weren't doing yourself any favours. You were making yourself a target.

But Peckham stayed with us when we ventured outside the area too. Being from there, it was risky to visit areas like Brixton, Lewisham or the Old Kent Road. Even if you had family there, you weren't welcome. You might *not* die, but then again you *might*. It didn't matter who you were, but it mattered where you were from. Why there was animosity between these areas was beyond my understanding – it wasn't even worth asking the question. It had always been this way. And Peckham had a reputation, for good and for bad.

For such a small area, with a population of around 70,000, the name Peckham rang bells all over London and throughout the UK. It was no small thing that the rap scene was fast growing and back then we had – without doubt – the best rapper at the time, Giggs. We were big fans, and listened loyally to him and his rap group, SN1. If you had a phone with infrared, like my Nokia 6230, there was a high chance that you had a song on it from a Peckham Boy.

But Peckham was also notorious for the death of ten-year-old Nigerian schoolboy Damilola Taylor in 2000. He'd been found bleeding to death in a stairwell, stabbed in a random attack just moments after he had left Peckham Library after school. His killers, only teenagers themselves at the time, didn't go to prison until six years later, and Damilola's innocent face flashed up on national news reports for a long time afterwards.

As far as we were concerned, fear us, love us, or hate us – the point was, you'd heard of us.

Like the time I went with my friend Naeem, who I knew through football, and his mate Shaun to visit Shaun's cousin. This was before I was tight with Femi, before I was tight with Dwayne. Naeem and Shaun lived in the same block, about a ten-minute bike ride from me, but Shaun's cousin lived in south-west London, where we knew Peckham Boys weren't welcome. On the bus there, we were joking around as usual – giving Naeem grief about his big nose. 'Oh my days . . . it's like a shotgun!' we were laughing. I guess it was our way of deflecting the stress. We just needed to stay cool, and get in and out of this area that wasn't ours in one piece. The afternoon was young, and the sun shone brightly: white T-shirt and white Air Force 1s weather. Everyone was making the most of this opportunity to bring out their summery outfits, just the odd guy here and there who didn't feel the heat enough to give up his puffer or hoodie – the uniform on our south London streets.

We pressed the bell at our stop and, stepping off the bus, it was like switching realms. We adjusted our behaviour accordingly. No joking around with each other now. We walked with purpose, keeping our heads down. We'd nearly made it, just a few minutes away from Shaun's cousin's house, a road or two to go, when our luck changed. Two older guys blocked the path in front of us. They were both Black, at least in their twenties – so much older than us – and dressed in tracksuits with jackets zipped all the way up. They must have been boiling. One of them had a very long and full beard. Our hood radars blinked. We braced ourselves.

'Yo, what ends are you man from fam?' they said, approaching us. That infamous, always unwanted question. A wrong answer here could get you an arse-whipping or, worse, stabbed. My head flooded with thoughts. Had someone recognized us from somewhere? A rap video on YouTube, perhaps? Did they know we weren't locals? Why would they approach us? But mostly: what did we do now?

We were off the main road and there was no one around. No witnesses. No Good Samaritans to step in and save us if we needed saving. We had two options. And in these situations, these were always the same options: stay and try to take them on. Or run. Suspicion alone wasn't enough to make us leg it. If we ran then we'd look guilty of something. Guilty of being from elsewhere.

'We're just visiting our friend who lives over there,' Shaun said, pointing vaguely to the direction of his cousin's house. *Thank God*, I thought, breathing silently in relief. Not the truthful answer, but the right answer. If we'd said what area we really were from then that would have made us a target. We were brave, for sure, but we weren't stupid, and Shaun had swerved the question successfully. We needed to be very careful about what we said.

'Do you have the time?' one of them asked.

'Nah, you know,' we all replied, shaking our heads.

Inside, I flinched. I could sense the mood shifting, and it felt as though we were heading into trouble. This didn't feel like a genuine question. Neither of these men looked in a rush. Neither of them needed to know the time. It was a trick, just like when Devon had asked to 'borrow my bike quickly'. The moment we revealed a watch or a phone, it would be gone.

Feeling nervous, but trying hard not to show it, I could see the worry written all over Naeem and

Shaun's faces, and hoped mine wasn't revealing the same. But it couldn't be helped, they looked defeated. We all knew what was coming. Without any words passing between us, we knew these guys were going to try and rob us.

They asked our names. We told them, still trying to hold our ground. Safety was just two roads away.

'Naeem, yeah, that's a Muslim name?' the bearded guy responded. 'Are you Muslim, yeah?' His face broke with a slight smile, as if he had met one of his brothers.

'Yeah, yeah,' Naeem said. It was a lie, of course, he was lying through his teeth, but he'd spotted the opportunity.

Naeem was as religious as Richard Dawkins. He may have had a Muslim name, but in no way was he a practising Muslim. But who was I to judge? I was all for whatever could get us out of this predicament. I was sure God would forgive him for whatever lies he needed to tell. If these men saw Naeem as one of their Muslim brothers, they might decide to leave us alone.

The long-bearded guy fist-bumped Naeem. 'Assalamu alaikum,' he said. *Peace be unto you*. Then, he raised an eyebrow expectantly.

Naeem echoed the words back, 'Assalamu alaikum,' like the complete idiot he was.

Even Shaun and I, who were raised in Christian

households, knew that you were meant to reply, 'Wa-Alaikum-Salaam'. *And unto you peace.* But Naeem, the supposed follower of Islam, didn't have a clue.

In that moment, he had ruined the slim chance we had of turning events around.

As I was still registering Naeem's error, there was a *thwack!* – the long-bearded guy slapped Naeem for his disrespectful lie. Then, as me and Shaun stood pinned to the spot, he led Naeem a few metres away. They were still in sight of us, and we looked on fearfully. These guys might have been Muslim, but they were most definitely not on their holy *deen*.

'You got a phone?' the other guy asked me.

'I ain't got a phone with me,' I replied, turning out my pockets to prove that they were empty. My phone was in a secret pocket down in my tracksuit bottoms, near my lower thigh. I had put it there earlier; but I hadn't known it would be such a lifesaver.

Then he turned to Shaun, who was not as fortunate. He was wearing the wrong trousers that day. His phone was clearly visible, and the guy just took it – though he gave him back his sim card as a kind gesture. Naeem had been led maybe ten or fifteen paces in front. We heard the long-bearded guy murmur something we couldn't make out, but we watched as Naeem brought out his phone too and handed it over. All of this happened without a fight or struggle. Three of us, two of them. I was fuming that we couldn't just take them on.

Afterwards, we made our way to Shaun's cousin's, trying to cling on to the day, but the energy had shifted. We weren't really in the mood. It was a close shave, and we were just innocent guys trying to enjoy the hot weather and visit a friend like anyone else. Trawling back home defeated, quiet now on the bus home, I knew this moment had changed me.

What I learned was this: I never wanted to be in that situation again. It was sickening. And here's the thing: it was ego-crushing to think that some-one saw me as easy prey, to get a free phone or a watch. That when they looked at me, what they saw was a victim. I couldn't have people thinking that they could take my stuff from me, and that I would just let them. These men didn't manage to strip me of my phone that day, but they did strip away my pride. This type of life couldn't be my story.

Life in the hood forced my hand. I had to be strong, as the weak get devoured. I didn't want to get robbed for my possessions or get stabbed or shot, and I certainly didn't want to die. I know there's a saying that 'only the good die young', but I wanted to live long, and I wanted to live well. If I had to be bad to die old, then so be it. In the hood, there were boys like me with the faces of dead friends printed on their T-shirts, a constant reminder of what could happen if you didn't step up. I decided that I would do whatever it took not to be that face with the letters R.I.P. written below it. Wouldn't you do the same?

The life expectancy for the average teenager living in the UK today is eighty-seven.[1] Yet for a thirteen-year-old Kenny, even with my whole life ahead of me, I would have been proud to see twenty-one. In this war zone, all of the younger Peckham Boys had to fight battles we had inherited from the generations before us, plus the new ones we started ourselves. You couldn't call yourself a Peckham Boy and refuse to be drafted in. Everyone had to play their part in this small but mighty army. And the price you might pay to be a part of it was always at the back of our minds.

Besides, it worked to my advantage to be affiliated with the most violent of Peckham's troublemakers and moneymakers, the Dwaynes and Femis of this world. Being friends with them offered me VIP protection and some form of immunity. This didn't mean I would avoid problems, or that I was free to disrespect or violate whoever I liked. I couldn't. But it meant that a lot of unfortunate things that happened to others wouldn't happen to me. I knew that, under their protection, I would no longer be a prime target for people in my hood to rob, disrespect, or bully. I also knew that if someone disrespected me, then Dwayne and Femi would smash in their head for me, or worse. They weren't bullies, far from it. But they would be for me. I only had to ask. Once I had them in my life, I couldn't imagine my life without them. There's nothing worse than growing up as a young kid in the hood with no brothers, cousins, or 'olders' to have your back.

I had a decision to make. I either owned being a Peckham Boy or I didn't. To people living outside of Peckham, and to my friends at school, many of whom came from other areas, I was one of them anyway, simply because of where I lived. Besides, I figured that you couldn't live here and be respected if you hadn't earned your stripes by doing your bit for the side. I was fed up with living and feeling like some nobody – the same nobody that watched his two friends get robbed and could do nothing about it. I had to learn to stand on my own two feet and stand my ground. I couldn't be a neek or a nerd. Some pushover. Some victim. Yet, there was also a part of me that knew better than to risk my life and my future for the glory of an area my family had no real stake in. My mother didn't own her house. She had no assets in the community other than her belongings piled high in every room. What would I be defending? What would I be fighting for?

It came down to this: if I was a Peckham Boy, at least my little brother George could have a different life. George looked up to me and I knew that, even at times when he was my shadow, my annoying little brother, he was all I had. Like any nine-year-old, he was mischievous and curious, always wanting to follow me to meet whoever I was meeting. But I didn't want him to have the same worries and experiences as me. I thought if I could do all the dirty work, he could enjoy a clean life. He could enjoy the sort of protection I had always longed for, before Dwayne and Femi took me under their wing. George could live his life differently and make better decisions. He could have options and choices about who his friends were. He could be a nerd and not have to worry about being bullied. His big brother would step in and resolve any conflicts. He would be in an even stronger position than me when I was his age.

If I could be my brother's keeper, life for him would be there for the taking. He just had one job to do – to live it as I said, and not as I did. This couldn't be that hard, right? But exactly what I had to do to become that person changed the trajectory of my life completely.

3

My New True Love

'The hottest love has the coldest end.' – Socrates

Love. It's a beautiful thing, they say. But what they don't tell you – or maybe you just don't listen when you're a teenager – is that love is only beautiful if you fall for the right person.

Call it puppy love if you like, but in my early teens I found my true love, but it wasn't a girl. It was the streets. It was the type of love every mother warns you about, begs you to stay away from. A dangerous love, irresistible love, a love that looks like trouble. But to me the streets were beautiful, the Delilah to my Samson. They promised me everything and more.

Despite all the warnings, I knew that as I continued to hang out with Dwayne and Femi, I was in it for the long haul: Till death do us part. So, I ignored every mother's warnings. Besides, I was broke, and this fact alone meant that I was overlooked by the real girls I might have wanted.

I was a smart kid. My grades were holding up well at school, but despite my teachers' promises of a place at university and a great job, this academic success was doing nothing for my pockets or my status. I was tired. Tired of wanting for more and tired of just surviving. The last thing I wanted to do was to beg my dad for money, or a laptop that would never materialize. And while my mum was doing her best, I had materialistic desires way beyond her shoestring budget. Like the Kickers I wanted for school. All the cool kids had them: shoes that announced themselves loudly with red and green tags to mark the right foot from the left so it was impossible to miss the label. Instead, I rocked up on my first day wearing black, boring Wallabees, and felt the shame bite with every step.

So all things considered, my love affair with the streets moved fast. I rushed forward and dived head first into this intense relationship. I was still just thirteen years old when I was presented with an opportunity to satisfy my greatest desire: to make real, tangible, spendable money.

It started like this: one day, during the neverending six-week summer holidays, I found myself sitting on a sofa in Camberwell with Femi. We were at his cousin Gloria's place, somewhere I had never been before. A couple of black dustbin bags were lying on the floor in the middle of the room. A particular smell was coming from them, a smell I knew too well. The whole room reeked of it, too overpowering for air freshener, too strong to mask or eliminate. It was weed. But this wasn't the small amounts I was used to seeing when my friends were chilling at home or at parties, carried just for personal use. This was half a kilo of cannabis.

Dwayne and Femi were pros at this game, but back then I was unfamiliar with the operation. They told me they bought the weed for a whole-sale price of around £2,000. To make a profit they planned to sell it separately to smokers in small amounts. Carefully, we had to prepare and package the product. And the recipe was simple: take one pack of see-through button bags and some cooking scales. Weigh up the weed on the scales, like you're preparing a cake mix. Then, push 1.5 grams of weed into each button bag and seal it shut. These bags are sold on for £10 each to weed smokers.

By this point, I'd been pestering Dwayne and Femi for months to employ me and help me make the money I desperately wanted. They hadn't let me in. 'Nah, bro,' they'd tell me. 'Defo not right now. When the time is right.' But that day there was more work than there were hands on deck. The weed had been offered to them unexpectedly and they'd jumped at the opportunity. I was one of the few people around they could trust and so, half-heartedly, they brought me in. For Dwayne and Femi, selling weed was low-risk compared to anything else I could sell for them, and it also meant I could get my money up, without relying on them and my mum. I joined the packing line: weighing, pushing, sealing, done. This job was no small feat. That afternoon we put together at least three hundred packs. It had been bright when we started, but the task took hours; the precision of weighing, the sheer heft of product we had to get through ran long into the evening.

Usually at my age, if you were selling weed on the streets you would start with a much smaller amount. Maybe fourteen grams (half an ounce), or twenty-eight if you're lucky. For me, this amount looked gigantic – something I'd only seen before in films – and enough to cover an average-sized coffee table, at least. These were big-time drug dealers I was working for, even if they were my older friends. By the time the street lights started glowing, we'd still not finished. We mounted up the small packs in a blue carrier bag in the corner and stopped for the day. All this weed would make us a £1,000 profit, and I would be able to pocket a third or more of it.

Despite my young age, I knew what I was doing. I wasn't naive. I knew the risks. Caught with all this weed, I could get a criminal record – or worse, be put in jail. As far as the justice system was concerned, I didn't know much, only what I'd learned from the streets. I had no real clue what happened to young offenders, but I'd heard of enough young people sent down for real time. I figured that at thirteen years old, I might be old enough to be put behind bars if a judge wasn't lenient. But a voice in my ear also kept reassuring me. It was full of justifications: 'It's just weed, Kenny. Not crack. Ain't nobody going to die from smoking a spliff.'

Or: 'Everybody smokes weed, right? From young people to key workers, to judges, to celebrities and politicians.'

Or: 'It's just Class C. You'll only get a slap on the wrist and a warning if you're caught with a few bags. You won't be going to jail unless they find all of it on you, which won't happen.'

When I was at my most anxious it always came back to this: 'If I'm lucky, I'll just get sent to a youth offending team, get given some community service. I won't go to jail. I'll just convince the judge that it would ruin my future.' It works for the White kids, right? Why shouldn't it work for me?

'Thanks for that, bro, I know it was a lot,' Dwayne told me that night. My chest puffed with pride. I liked every moment of being part of a production line, and hoped they would invite me again.

'When do we start moving it?' I asked, desperate to watch how the next part of the operation worked.

'Tonight . . .'

Later that evening, not only did Dwayne and Femi bring me along to their customers, but they promised to let me out on my own. Then, a couple of days later they gave me some money to buy a mobile phone and a new sim card – what we call a business line – for this new business venture, and a bicycle to get around – the same bike I got a busted lip for. They were both highly experienced and had mastered their craft. They could shift weed, cocaine, crack, you name it, and do it effortlessly. Keen as I was, I wasn't keen enough to get involved in anything other than weed. At that young age, a sixth sense told me this was as far as my risk threshold could take me – for now at least. But knowing the jungle I was about to enter into, they prepared me nonetheless. Dwayne and Femi taught me everything I needed to know. Weed was small change to them. In fact, they were happy to outsource that part of the operation to me.

Firstly, they introduced me properly to the customers I would be selling to, and they also passed my business number on to potential new customers. Secondly, they gave me helpful advice about how to thrive in the workplace and in the industry, as if I was the newest office intern wide-eyed and eager to learn on the job. 'Don't grab the attention of any community heroes who might snitch,' they told me, and this meant never talking about my work to anyone. They instilled a healthy paranoia in me about the police, and how I was to use various techniques to mask my illegal activities, such as giving people weed in discreet places like the stairwell of a block. I had to live another life, one of secrecy. No one apart from the people buying from me needed to know what I was doing. And the most important lesson: don't be too flashy, or hang around people who were known by everyone to sell drugs either. Never end up guilty by association.

Dwayne and Femi taught me a lot, but one thing they never had to teach me about was a work ethic. I already knew how to work hard. I'd seen how many hours my mother put in to make sure that me and my brother were provided for – and I brought that same dedication to my work too. Once everyone knew I was open for business, trade picked up quickly. The weed was high quality and that meant demand for it was also high. My customers kept me active. I would pedal miles up and down on my bike to make my sales. I cycled across Peckham, along to Camberwell, up the Walworth Road headed towards central London. In the other direction, I had regulars in Brockley and powered up hills to reach Crystal Palace, deep into south-east London. And whenever the voice in the back of my head had doubts, the streets pulled me back. I told myself: 'It's all good exercise, this pedalling up and down London. It's fitness training for football too, a win-win situation: money and muscles.' And I was good at it too.

In a matter of weeks, I'd sold half a kilo, courtesy of Dwayne and Femi's networks. I brought an entrepreneurial spirit to my probation period: while I was making sale after sale, I was also attracting and signing up more customers. My clientele was diverse too: White, Black, young, old, blue-collared workers, high status professionals, the rich and the poor. Exactly the same range of people you might see in your local Tesco Express. There were those who answered the door still in their work suits and others who looked messy, like all they did was smoke, eat and sleep. The haves and the have-nots – they all wanted to buy. Satisfied customers led to recommendations, recommendations meant more clients, and my network grew. No marketing beats word of mouth and the word was spreading about me fast.

When all the weed in Gloria's house had been sold, there was more where that came from. And I craved more. Thanks to my training, I had become confident in my ability, and having done so well as

a worker for Dwayne and Femi I became convinced that I could run this business by myself. It
was straightforward enough. The infrastructure
was all there to expand and scale, and I was a fast
learner, ready to run even though I'd just started
walking. Learning the game from the best of the
best made me feel unstoppable.

Any good mentor knows that the goal is to
make your mentee self-sufficient. So when I
approached Dwayne and Femi about my ideas,
that I wanted to branch out with my own business
without their money and involvement, they gave
me their blessing. As I say, weed was small change
to them, and they were happy for me to be making
my own money.

'Just be smart,' Femi advised me. 'Remember
what we told you.' As a final favour they allowed
me to keep the work phone, packed with clients
and contacts, so I didn't have to start from scratch.
Just like that, their customers became my customers. Now, I was flying solo, with a head start on
many of my competitors. They were friends my
age who were also selling weed, but as small-timers
who didn't have the benefit of mentors and contacts. Nor did they have the same drive for success
that I'd found at such a young age. While they
were still in start-up mode, I had an established
business.

I'd made enough money from that first flip – the

initial money I'd earned with Femi and Dwayne – to buy my own weed wholesale. It was nowhere near the half a kilo I'd started with, but enough to get me going. Dwayne and Femi had introduced me to their suppliers too, and thanks to my affiliation with them I also had a great credit rating. Like Klarna, I could buy now and pay later. Business is business. No matter the industry, it all works the same.

Before long, my phone was ringing non-stop. There was no time to eat, barely time to sleep. My life was now spent adding up numbers and riding on my bike to meet clients. Like any great delivery start-up – Deliveroo, Uber Eats, one of those – I operated around the clock (when I wasn't in school, of course), and people could order from me at whatever time they pleased. Fast asleep in bed, dreaming, I'd wake up to the sound of my mobile ringing and jump up, ready for the working day. I'd get dressed, hop on my bike, and make the delivery, sneaking quietly and guiltily out of the house while Mum and George slept. People could choose 'click and collect' and meet me near where I was based, like the car park around the corner or deep in the estate opposite, or have it delivered to an address of their choice. My customer service was flawless. I prided myself on it, in fact.

Hustling on the streets quickly put me in a position where I had more disposable income than my mum, than most of my friends' parents even. The work wasn't honest, but it was justly rewarding. I felt like a self-made success – a real man. Working the streets pushed me out of my comfort zone and stretched me. It encouraged me to make even more money. And I adored all the new-found riches I had earned. I loved my fresh designer clothes and looking good in the latest shoes that cost almost half of my mother's monthly rent. I had binned my black boring Wallabees, walked straight down to Rye Lane to get the Kickers I'd wanted so badly, and it felt sweeter knowing I had earned the money to buy them myself.

Making money and earning my stripes meant I was becoming the somebody I had long desired to be. I was a lot more confident now. Not that I was shy before, but a shoebox full of money has its way of giving you that extra spring in your step. I was also becoming more popular, and I lapped up the attention that came my way. Before, I was just another guy, to girls, but now those who had never looked my way in the past responded to me differently, and I knew how to reel them in. I enjoyed flirting, and got a thrill from competing with friends to see how many we could sleep with. I'm not proud of it now, but I had a different girl every week, almost at the same speed at which I had new clothes or trainers. Money came first and girls came second, but I always knew money got me girls, too. But the minute I got too distracted, the streets pulled me back. Reminded me I needed to work, not waste my time and money on girls.

A few months in, on a day when my legs hadn't stopped moving from the moment I woke up to the moment I hit the pillow, I realized demand was more than my workforce of one could deliver. It was time to expand the business. But who could I trust? I discreetly asked around. My friend Damson put himself forward first. I had known him since childhood, and knew that he could benefit from the same perks I was enjoying. He talked a good game, and we had fun taking the piss out of each other. 'Trust me, bro,' he said. 'I've got this.' He gave me this whole spiel about how keen he was to work for me and how he'd be so good at the job, and how desperate he was to make real money, which I could understand.

So, I gave him a chance, as you do with friends. This lazy fool didn't last a day! He quit after a few hours, bumbling through excuses about why he'd have to resign, effective immediately. In his exit interview he told me that he was overwhelmed by the busyness of the job. He also suffered from a health condition called sickle cell, that several of my other friends in the Black community also lived with. An abnormality in the body's red blood cells, its symptoms, like seizures, are severe, and in some cases life-threatening. Damson got tired more easily than other people. He spent spells in hospital and I guess he didn't want to take any risks, no matter how enticing the lure of easy money was. It's safe to say this profession wasn't for everyone.

Me, I was a natural – or at least that's what I told myself. The only problem was that despite reaping the fruits of my labour, I was still only a teenager, and this was my first job. On my own, the business became unsustainable. Money came in fast but it disappeared fast as well. I wasn't managing my money well, and there was no incentive not to run the business dry. I was not accountable to anyone, so I just spent my income how I liked. When I realized I had blown through all of my revenue, and that there was no more cash flow to keep going and buy new product with, I had to close the shop. I had failed, as most people do with their first business. But just when I thought it was all over I found my first business partner: Levelle. He was also a funny guy, intelligent too, and we went to the same school. We had known each other since primary school and he lived less than a five minute walk away from my area.

'Bruv, I'm so low, I need more paper,' I said to him one day while we were chilling. I'd taken a look at my savings and realized they were almost at zero.

'Me too, bro, we need to change our situation.

Bring me in,' he pleaded. Like me, he wanted to earn a good living. Also, he was nothing like Damson. Levelle's work ethic did not compare, so I knew he would be as invested in this business as me.

'I know a way we can make some serious money, but I don't have enough to start,' I told him. I would need some investment to get up and running again, and then we could build the business back up.

The next day Levelle came to me with his last fifty pounds, one bright pink £50 note to ensure my business kept rolling. With his seed money on the table, I brought him on-board as an equal part-ner, training him up and making sure he knew how the current infrastructure operated. We worked together to meet demand and shared the work shifts. We shared the profits too, 50/50.

Soon I passed the milestone of saving my first £1,000, an amount that my mum, despite her mul-tiple jobs and careful spending, could never have done after she'd paid out her weekly or monthly bills. Counting through my earnings, flipping the tens and twenties through my fingers, I couldn't make sense of it. How could I make this much money at my age, but my mum could work so hard for years and still have nothing? I felt proud that I no longer had to be her financial burden, but there was a strange guilt attached to it too. The imbalance seemed unfair. As a courtesy, I would still ask her if I could buy something, but it was only out of politeness. I no longer needed her permission, I had all the funds myself. To cover up, I would say that anything expensive I owned was a gift, or bought with the money I made from doing odd jobs in the community – odd jobs indeed. This would also explain all my running around and strange activities, I thought.

The grip my mum had over me was loosening, and she could tell. I'd catch her studying me silently as we passed through the corridor of our shared home, wondering when it was that she'd lost control of her son. I no longer sought validation from her. I was breaking her rules and constantly pushing her boundaries as well as her patience. As I got deeper into the streets, my curfew got broken so regularly that we stopped arguing outside the front door. There was no point in it. Despite all her sacrifices, best efforts, and empty threats that if I kept misbehaving I would be taken back to Nigeria, here I was, becoming my own man and making my own decisions. For better or worse, only time would tell, but I was too young and too arrogant to care.

Most painfully for her, the message about being careful of the friends I chose had fallen on deaf ears. My friendship circle was unrecognizable from before. I was now repping Peckham proudly with my chest; *this* was my home and I belonged here. I now had another family, and by embracing them I became much of what my mother had always feared for me: I was your stereotypical Peckham Boy. I had criminals, drug dealers and violent offenders for mates. I was spending more time with people who were more likely to lead me to a prison cell or a coffin, instead of a university graduation ceremony or a high-flying corporate job. Occasionally, I did find myself in police custody for a few hours at Peckham or Walworth Road. I was never charged with anything – and at the end of the day, business was still operating nicely without interference from authorities – but what can I say? Law enforcement seemed to like my company. But my mother's dream boy was becoming her nightmare. I was selling drugs and, smart with it as I was, good at it or not, trouble was bound to follow.

The thing is, to run a business like mine, people had to know I wasn't a pushover, or an easy target, that I wasn't 'that guy'. I wasn't that guy you could trouble easily, or the weakest link in the group to target. I wasn't that guy you would think to rob if you were low on money and wanted to kidnap a drug dealer. I wasn't that guy you could hold up in the street and demand a phone, a bike, or *anything* from. Not any more. The same Kenny that couldn't defend himself or stand his ground was gone. And to prove it, I knew I had to get my hands dirty. I let people know I was happy to work with my fists, and anything I could grab, and get my hands bloody.

Late one evening, travelling home after a day of non-stop deliveries, I made a quick stop at McDonald's so that I could finally eat. It was a simple mission, in and out before I got back to work. But on my way to the counter I passed three guys. 'We hit the belly,' I heard one of them say, and my ears pricked up. That meant they'd hit the jackpot. I knew if I played it right, there was money to be made for myself. They went on discussing how much cash they'd come into, but I couldn't make out how. I paused, just listening, hovering next to them while their lips ran loose. When they walked out, so did I.

'Come around the corner, let me talk to you,' I told them. My stare was strong. I read their hesitance like a book, saw them gulp but try to hide it. Nothing in the hood is ever what it seems, so we all knew that the one thing I didn't want to do was 'talk'. Whether it was through fear, I don't know, but they followed me to a discreet location behind McDonald's, and when the four of us were alone I pulled out a canister of CS gas that I'd concealed under my clothing.

'Pass over whatever you got fam,' I said viciously. I didn't have to ask twice; they knew I wasn't there for a polite conversation. CS gas leaves victims choking, their eyes burning. The sort of weapon that should never be in people's hands, yet for Peckham Boys it was carried as common protection, as were knives and even baseball bats – and for a few, guns. Without hesitation, they handed over all the money they'd just made from whatever crime they'd committed. It was around £500. They didn't want any trouble, just like Shaun, Naeem and I when we were younger. These guys had made their calculations, and realized this was the easiest and safest way for them to get out of the situation. The only difference was these weren't little boys, these were kids my age. I was outnumbered, and they could have tried to jump me. But you see fear, and once it grips people, they're paralysed.

This was the Kenny I had become.

But this wasn't *all* that I was. On the flip side, I was still a star student. Despite the life I was living outside of school hours, I still had a vision, I still had dreams. Somewhere in the back of my mind, I knew that my mother had not travelled all this way for me to end up mediocre, and I was certain that my success at making money was proof that there were no limits to what I could achieve. My mum was banking on me being a big success, and after everything I was putting her through I was determined she cashed out.

I guess to some people I was a very successful illegal pharmacist, providing medication in the form of cannabis across the capital. To other people, especially teachers, I was a bright Black boy and butter wouldn't melt in my mouth. But balancing business and school became a risky operation. During the day, I would put on my school uniform: white shirt, black trousers, black blazer with an iron-on badge. By night, I would dress for work: dark tracksuit with the trousers tucked into my socks so they wouldn't catch in my bike chain. By day, I would study diligently and, at the end of the day, I would turn straight to my business phone.

Most of my clients worked an honest 9 to 5, so their schedules aligned with mine. After school and weekends were the times when people really needed their packages, though on occasion I was known to arrive at school late if I had early morning orders to fulfil. My classmates were none the wiser and I intended to keep it that way, giving myself a rule that I would never sell to them and they would never know.

But while none of them knew about my drugs business, they didn't see me as a nerd either. To them I was a fighter and a hustler when I needed to be. Yes, I presented well and got good grades, but I was also the boy who, on his lunch break, would make extra cash by selling contraband snacks:

Capri-Suns and jam doughnuts and Rocky bars –
all the items that it was strictly prohibited to sell in
the playground. I never picked fights, or sought
out trouble, but it was known I could hold my
own – but only after the bell had rung, and far
away from the school gates if a score needed to be
settled.

That's why what happened next was a real shock.
I'd been sat among my year group in the school's
egg-shaped auditorium, in complete silence as our
head of year Mrs Logan started speaking. She was
small in stature but not in voice, which she projected loudly as she ran through the names of every
student chosen to become a junior prefect that year.
That was a big deal. The school hadn't had junior
prefects before and successful students would get a
badge and become apprentices to the prefects in
Years 10 and 11. We clapped politely after each
name was called. Most of them were the usual suspects, the well-behaved and book-smart kids. No
surprises there. Then suddenly, everybody heard
Mrs Logan say the words: 'Kenny Imafidon.'

Me? A junior prefect? It didn't seem real. My
eyes widened, surprise all over my face. I hadn't
seen that one coming! Looking around the auditorium, I was confronted with a sea of faces whose
expressions matched my own: filled with astonishment. They began to clap hesitantly, as everyone
watched me rock up from my seat.

The other students weren't saying it out loud but I could almost hear them muttering under their breath, 'Him of all people.' I walked to the end of my row and strolled towards Mrs Logan confidently, taking my time to soak up the moment and the applause. I joined the handful of other students to celebrate becoming the school's first-ever junior prefects. Who would have thought it? Kenny Imafidon, a role-model student by day, a drug dealer by night. What a life.

And, if truth be told, I was, on paper at least, a shining example to others and a poster boy for my school. On several occasions, I had been elected by my classmates to be the class representative on the school council. This meant I had to deliver everyone's views to the senior leadership team and discuss ideas about changes and improvements to the school. I was *good* at all this, but even by my reasoning, becoming a junior prefect was a step up I wouldn't have thought possible. And if you'd asked my real friends, they'd have laughed at the idea.

Clearly my teachers weren't aware of what was going on behind the scenes. But by now I was well-practised in the art of deception – a chameleon. They'd have had no clue about the fights I'd been having after school, just a few minutes' walking distance from the school gates. They knew nothing about my reputation as a Peckham Boy, and all

I was doing out of sight. In fact, teachers seemed to warm to me, and although I didn't always feel the same way about them, there were two brilliant teachers who I liked, respected and listened to, and who did have a positive impact on me.

One of them was Mr Johnson, a fairly middle-aged White man, who went to a top Russell Group university. I wasn't in his class, but I used to talk to him if I was ever waiting for Levelle at the end of lessons. He was someone who took an interest in me and gave me the time of day. He would engage me in discussions about famous philosophers like Socrates and Immanuel Kant. At times Mr Johnson, Levelle and I would debate philosophical questions about ethics, and utilitarianism versus deontology. I'd give Mr Johnson scenarios which we could talk about. I remember once I asked him: 'If you are driving a car, would you swerve and kill one person to avoid killing four others?' This led on to a deep conversation about whether doing one bad thing for the greater good was okay. He was one of a few people who really sparked my interest to learn more about philosophy, and also inspired me to believe I could study what he had studied.

There was also Mrs Chambers, a no-nonsense Black Caribbean teacher and assistant headteacher. She was the type of person who, if you misbehaved in class, would call your parents there and then, in front of everybody – which nobody wanted, myself included. She was a graduate from one of the country's top five universities. She pushed me to do double science and to believe that I could really go to one of the best universities in the world, like she did.

But inside I was always caught between two worlds. As I stood accepting my new prefect position, my mind flashed back to the previous week. Me and Babatunde, a friend of mine even though he was from Brixton, were sat in our final lesson of the day. Bored and eager for the bell to ring, we'd both been making fun of each other in our PSHE class. It was light-hearted at first, but one of his jokes crossed a line.

'Shut up!' I told him, but he was unapologetic.

'No, your mum can shut up!' he laughed back. Any mention of anyone's mum could start big fights at my school.

Diss me, but don't bring my mum into it, I thought.

'Just watch,' I told him.

'Watch what?' he kept saying, prodding at me. 'I ain't scared of you, bruv.' He was talking heavy, like he thought he was Wladimir Klitschko or something. But I was no longer playing with him. I held my tongue. I was silent for the rest of the class, and soon so was he. It was unspoken, but we both knew that the moment school-Kenny had clocked off and streets-Kenny had clocked in, we were going to get it cracking. I wasn't about to let a puppy like him, who wouldn't even survive a day where I came from, get too big for his boots and step up to a young lion like me. If I didn't deal with him swiftly then other puppies might think they could follow suit. The argument may have seemed over a small thing but he had disrespected me. My reputation was on the line here and I was not going to lose it all because of Babatunde.

As soon as class was over and the teacher – who was just as eager to leave as us – disappeared from view, I was off like a greyhound at a racing track. I ran towards Babatunde and knocked him senseless with left and right hooks to his head and temple. Our fight was quick and if anybody did stay behind to see the action, they would have wasted their time. A surge of adrenaline tore through me as I pounded him to the floor. He seemed pathetic and helpless. Only your parents should be able to beat you the way I beat him that day.

On reflection, this fight, alongside many others I had back then, would have been seen by outsiders as pointless, and could have been prevented. But once my ego or pride was bruised, fighting seemed like the only solution. And I always knew I would get away with it. I was smart that way. My school was too focused on the students who disrupted lessons, missed classes, or who displayed behavioural issues. That wasn't me. Teachers weren't looking at students like me, hiding in plain sight. It was an

Oscar-worthy performance, these two different versions of Kenny, each tailored to different people. Denzel Washington or Leonardo DiCaprio had nothing on me.

But just because it was an act, it doesn't mean that it wasn't real. In truth, I wasn't trying to trick my teachers – for my mum and for myself, I was committed to my school responsibilities. For teachers, that was a breath of fresh air in a state school like mine; a school notorious for things that had nothing to do with brilliant grades and outstanding Ofsted ratings. It was not a school to which parents were in any rush to send their children. There were no waiting lists or entrance exams. Whenever its name was mentioned it was always about how rough it was, and that students were stabbed inside and outside of the gates. Before I'd even got there, it had been put on special measures due to poor performance, and the fact that only 15 per cent of students were achieving five GCSEs (A*–C) was not helped by the fact that almost three hundred exclusions were put in place in one school year.

Going to this school was nothing to be proud of. In fact, the junior prefect role had been created to tackle this poor reputation and change the school ethos into something that, on paper, looked more promising. Yet I witnessed a lot of violence and bullying taking place, and it took various forms. On a typical day a group of the older guys might force people who walked into the boys' toilets to do the 'YMCA' dance, just to make fools out of them. Scared individuals either agreed and danced, or froze to the spot, mentally preparing themselves for the beating if they resisted.

You would also see the same old repeat offenders bunking classes and using their new-found free time to gamble and play 'pound up' all day – perfecting the skill of throwing pound coins to land as close to the wall as possible, as though that's what matters in life. And the threat of violence was lurking everywhere. You had to be wary even if you just had a nice phone: that could get stolen inside school. And fear meant you wouldn't tell the teachers about it either.

From the moment I stepped through its doors I knew that the rumours about this school hadn't come from nowhere. The majority of students in our school were from Black African and Caribbean backgrounds, living in poverty and facing multiple challenges. There was no real sense of aspiration. I may have had hopes and dreams and plans, and my mum had certainly instilled in me that getting a decent education would help me achieve them. But I was in the minority.

The bitter coincidence, particularly for someone like me, was that a stone's throw away was an independent all-boys' school with a long-standing reputation for producing some of the nation's well-known musicians, actors, sportsmen, writers, politicians, journalists and judges. It was a school that cost over £7,000 a term to attend, and more if you were boarding. Today, the boarding fees would be around £44,000 a year. In this elite environment, students were being trained to become future leaders. They learned all that we did and more, but what their fees were really paying for was self-confidence, and some may even say entitlement. It was drummed into them. From the outset, they learned that the odds were in their favour and that their life was more or less mapped out for them. And so was mine . . .

I would never have known it growing up, but I've since looked at the statistics. What we were feeling every day – that the odds were stacked against kids like us, who attended state schools, from the start – is there in black and white. In the UK, only 7 per cent of the population attend private schools, yet 39 per cent of the top jobs in society are taken up by people who went to fee-paying schools. That's 29 per cent of our elected MPs, 65 per cent of our senior judges, 43 per cent of the hundred most influential news editors and broadcasters, and 48 per cent of CEOs of FTSE 350 companies, who have all been privately educated. Even in sports, where we believe success is about pure talent, private school kids dominate. In the Tokyo 2020 Olympics, 35 per cent of British medal winners were privately educated for at least some of their secondary school life.

When everyone around you is flourishing, how could you not feel confident about your future? How could you not believe it's possible to grow up and be the Prime Minister one day, if you attend Eton College where twenty of Britain's fifty-seven prime ministers have also attended?

Our school had no alumni of importance, as far as I knew. We had no track record of producing any of the country's future leaders or top earners. The expectations placed on us, compared to those students, were incomparable. For some, just getting five or more GCSEs and not leaving school pregnant was a success. We could only dream of being in an atmosphere of learning, and enjoying the enrichment opportunities provided to the kids next door. The difference in our life chances was astronomical. We were physically close, but our lives couldn't have been further apart. Some people try to fight against those inequalities, but many just surrender. It takes energy to keep fighting on such an uneven playing field. (Coincidentally, the playing fields were the only thing we shared with the kids next door – they allowed us to use theirs, but I imagine they weren't too happy about it.)

When our teams walked past each other it was obvious we came from different worlds: them, White boys dressed in brand new uniforms. Us, a group of mostly Black boys, dressed in whatever kit we could find that morning. The only thing we had on them was that our Nike and adidas branded shoes were cleaner than the lesser-known brands on their feet.

I often wondered about their lives, and as my business started to grow I felt encouraged by the thought that right now, maybe my pockets were just as fat as theirs. Unlike the average teenager, I could shop in luxury department stores like Selfridges. And if I'd wanted to, I could also have eaten in the finest restaurants, whose dishes I probably wouldn't have been able to pronounce, and bought excessively overpriced bottles at parties, even though I wasn't old enough to drink. I wasn't even old enough to drive, but I could have bought my first car if I'd wanted to, though it would have been nothing like Dwayne's or Femi's. And I could do all of this without the bank of Mum and Dad, unlike the super-privileged millennials I saw around me.

I wasn't the only one prospering, either. My friends were getting richer by the day too. Not everyone was good at selling drugs, but those that were made good money. Often, I would bump into them shopping in designer clothes stores like Colors in Peckham, or flagship designer stores in the West End. Besides, what could we really do with the money? It's not as if we could save for mortgages with drug money. Most of us sold weed, but some sold crack cocaine, wanting that big money that weed couldn't get you. Either way, we were all on the hustle and committed to making a million. It was the hood dream – even though we personally never knew anyone who had made that yet. Dwayne and Femi were rich, but certainly not millionaires.

And that would always be the difference. I'm sure the students at that school next door, who were as smart as me, weren't living a double life and selling weed in their spare time. I'm sure any money they had wasn't stuffed away in discreet places where it couldn't be found by parents or authority figures. Those students could live free of fear of any real threats of violence, unnecessary harm or falling victim to a crime – at least not on their school premises. In state schools like mine, teachers couldn't provide the same learning environment. But as those teachers who did look out for me, and who did inspire me will tell you, it wasn't necessarily their fault. When the system throws thirty or more kids into a small and badly resourced classroom, it's the lack of funding for books, trips – even teachers – anything that might enrich our experience, that degrades the learning environment. It's the lack of support for newly trained teachers who are ill-equipped to work with students with complex needs. It's the lack of backing for students who need more personalized learning support but who can't access it.

So, of course, you could find yourself being told by your frustrated and burned-out teachers that you were destined to become a nobody and could end up working in McDonald's. The teachers don't have time for confidence building. Or for telling us we could be a person of status in the world. The way I see it, we could have lived with the privilege and advantages of the 7 per cent any day, but they wouldn't have lasted two minutes living with our poverty and disadvantage.

Who knows, maybe if I'd gone to a different school, like the one next door, and had the opportunities those students had, I might not have got caught up in this double life. But by then, even if I'd wanted to get out, the streets always found a way of catching up with me.

4

A Product of My Environment?

'Of course, as someone once observed, there is no right way to do something wrong.'
— Frank W. Abagnale, *Catch Me If You Can*

BOOM!

All I could see were the barrels of machine guns aimed at my body.

'Don't move! Armed police!'

They had kicked in the front door, sending it spinning off its hinges, and before I could even sit up in bed they were inside the room, ready to shoot if I made the wrong move.

'Put your hands in the air, where we can see them!'

I threw my hands up, like I was trying to touch the ceiling.

This was a surprise visit. A drugs raid is *always* a

surprise visit. This was Dayo's house, another friend I often chilled with. I'd spent the evening before hanging out, playing *Pro Evolution Soccer* on the PlayStation with him and his little brother Dami. Hours rolled into each other and I'd ended up sleeping over. The sun was yet to rise when the police stormed in. Wrong place, wrong time. Just my luck.

I stood as still as a guard outside Buckingham Palace, waiting as they patrolled the room. It was too early for this. I knew that I had nothing illegal on me but I couldn't say the same for the other two. If there was anything in the house that might incriminate the three of us, I had no idea. Dayo and Dami had their arms up like mine. All of us frozen still. I was too shaken even to signal to them in case the armed officers interpreted my movements as some form of guilt or, worse, an opportunity to blow me away.

We were not exactly upstanding citizens. We all sold drugs, but Dami was greedier and more committed to this life. He never finished school and didn't see himself as academic. Selling drugs was his calling, he felt. He'd think nothing of dealing crack cocaine and heroin, something I never did. For me, the stakes were too high. Besides, I never wanted crack addicts bothering me on Rye Lane, especially if I was walking with my mum.

While Dami was the quieter of the brothers, Dayo was fearless with a hot temper. Dayo did most of the dirty work for Dami, and fought his battles for him. He was not a guy to cross, and I knew he'd earned respect from all the people he'd blooded up. Yet when we were introduced to each other, we just clicked. His family were Nigerian too, although he was Yoruba – from a different tribe. My family are from the Edo/Bini tribe. Nigeria has more than 250 tribes, all with their own customs and languages. We needed our common bonds more than ever now.

Hurriedly, an officer flashed up a warrant to search the property. Not wasting a moment, the others then began turning the whole house upside down. Pillows tugged from their cases, trainers shook out, the laces dangling. Dayo, Dami and I sat in silence. There'd been no time to get dressed so we quivered on the edges of our beds in our boxer shorts, careful to keep our hands visible at all times. Surrounded by armed officers, we listened to the crashes as police yanked open cupboards and drawers and toppled furniture. It felt like it was their sole task to intimidate us, with their *Call of Duty*-style weapons. My mind was ticking over: what were they looking for? Why all the guns? Did somebody set us up, or what? But most crucially: was I implicated?

Nervously, I waited for one of the officers to announce whether they'd found anything. I couldn't put it past Dayo or Dami to have drugs in the house, and whereas I'd only ever been in minor trouble with the police before, a raid like this was nothing new to them. Time dragged. The search continued. No news was good news, I thought. My heart raced, thumping hard in my chest.

A mean-mugging officer strode into the room, staring us down.

'We've found some scales here, who do they belong to?' he asked, eyeballing each of us and holding up the black scales in his hand. They had some white powder on them, and it certainly wasn't no self-raising flour. I knew, and he knew, exactly what those scales were for.

'Dunno,' said Dayo, shrugging his shoulders.

'I dunno,' said Dami.

'Dunno,' I echoed the two of them. But I was telling the truth. For me, at least, it really was a mystery who they belonged to. The officer scowled. Unimpressed by our denial, he escalated the matter.

'Please put on some clothes, you're all coming with us,' he said firmly. I scurried to throw on my black and red adidas tracksuit and black Superstars, while my mind continued to race: *coming to where, exactly? I haven't done anything. Why can't you all leave and let me go back to sleep?*

'Get up and turn around,' the same officer barked once we'd got dressed. Carefully, with guns still pointing in our direction, we stood and turned. They handcuffed us, our wrists pulled roughly and tightly together behind our backs. Then, the arresting officer launched into his well-rehearsed spiel. I could hear the delight in his voice: 'You are being arrested for conspiracy to supply Class A drugs. You do not have to say anything, but it may harm your defence if you do not mention, when questioned, something which you later rely on in court. Anything you do say may be given in evidence . . .'

Speech over, we were escorted downstairs and led outside the house with our shiny handcuffs on, paraded for anyone who was up early enough to watch. And they *were* watching, curtains twitching to see what was going on. I glanced back at the front door which had taken such a pounding that it was now completely broken, dangling off its hinges. To be frank, though, it had been in a bad way even before the police arrived, still scarred from the last time they booted it down some months back. And whenever that happened, Dayo and Dami's mum would have to pay to fix it, irrespective of whether they found anything in the house or not. It's not criminal damage if it's done by the police.

We filed into the van, heads bowed. I felt the hard seats and uncomfortable silence, the long and bumpy journey letting me know that we weren't being driven to one of our usual local police stations. Our final destination: Southwark Police

Station, near Elephant and Castle, towards central London.

I had never been to Southwark Police Station before, but I knew exactly what to expect: before they dashed me into a custody suite, to lie on a wooden bed with a rock-hard mattress and a toilet I wouldn't be using if I could help it, I would be reminded by an officer of my legal rights. Then, they'd recite why I had been arrested – as if I could forget! I'd thought about little else in the cold stillness of the van, feeling the cuffs digging into my skin. I would have to confirm my personal details before being led to have my mugshot taken and fingerprints scanned. Only after this would I be able to make a short phone call to one person to tell them where I was. I didn't plan on letting everyone know I was here today, especially not my mum.

As I was under eighteen, I couldn't be questioned in police custody without an appropriate adult being present. So I called Dwayne's little brother Jermaine, who was in his mid-twenties, to come to the station and sit in on my interview. Mum could only ever be my last resort, because I didn't even know how I could break it to her. The phone rang and I uttered a little prayer inside, hoping he would answer.

'Yo Jermaine, I just got nicked and need your help. I'm at Southwark Police Station. Can you come and get me?'

'Ahh for real?' he said, sounding a bit stunned. 'Give me twenty.'

I also knew from the handful of times I'd been arrested before that it was my legal right to have a solicitor represent me and give me free legal advice if I wanted it. I was certainly going to be agreeing to that. But it wasn't as if I'd ever had my own personal solicitor – I didn't have that type of money. Instead, I would be asking for a duty solicitor, an independent solicitor from a local law firm who was sent to me for free. Once he or she arrived, I would be able to speak with them privately. I sat impatiently in my custody suite, my stomach groaning with hunger. After all, I'd been rudely woken before breakfast and I refused to eat the 'food' offered to me at the station – some disgusting microwave meal that I would never eat at home. All that I could think about was that my solicitor, whoever they found for me, had better hurry up. I needed to get *out*. Every minute that ticked by in that cell reminded me of why I hadn't committed the crime and why I shouldn't be there.

When I'd been allowed to speak to him on the phone, the solicitor said he would be here ASAP, in an hour tops. But he took more like two, and by the time he arrived, Jermaine and I had run out of patience.

I had nothing to say to the police and nothing to say to my solicitor either, who didn't know how to keep to time, and didn't seem like he understood what the wait had been like for me. He briefly apologized, said he'd been held up, but moved on to business as usual. As I wasn't paying him for his services, I didn't pull him up on his lateness, but as far as I was concerned, all they needed to know was that I was innocent. I had nothing to own up to. The scales weren't mine and I didn't supply Class A drugs like crack or heroin. Besides, I knew they had no proof of either.

In a private interview room, the solicitor told me he'd already been briefed on the case and the alleged charges against me. Throughout my account of events leading to the arrest, I maintained my innocence and he believed me – or at least he smiled politely to make it look like he did.

Not long after, I was led out to be questioned by the two officers who had been part of the raid that morning, who had yanked me from sleep with their guns and their shouting. My solicitor was present too in the poorly lit interview room. It was grey with walls that looked like they were padded with some sort of soundproofing. One table sat in the middle of the room, with a few chairs scattered around, nothing warm or welcoming at all.

Our interview was quite short. I preferred it that way, too. I confirmed my name, and responded with 'no comment' to all the questions the officers asked me. It was my legal right not to answer any of their questions, if I chose. So I exercised my rights. I knew they had nothing on me, so I didn't sweat it. More than that, I could see my vow of silence was winding the officers up, which gave me a bit of satisfaction. I just needed to get released on bail or, even better, have the case against me dropped. I felt confident my chances of getting one of those two outcomes were extremely high given the circumstances.

After the interview, the officers put me back in my custody suite while they finished up Dayo's and Dami's interviews. I waited and waited, wondering what was taking everybody so long. I knew the brothers would never lie and say the scales were mine, or get me in any trouble. We were brothers – as loyal to each other as soldiers in the Navy SEALs.

As I sat there, the sound of footsteps got louder and louder and suddenly I could hear keys jingling. An officer flung open my creaky door.

'Your solicitor wants to see you,' he said before leading me down the corridor to where the duty solicitor was now waiting.

He looked up and smiled. 'You're getting bail.' I would have no other conditions to comply with, other than returning to the station in a month or so. But, for now at least, the stress was over. I was free. Hopefully Dayo and Dami would get bail too, I thought, and hoped my solicitor could tell me their fate.

'I don't know about your friend Dayo yet,' he

said. 'But your friend Dami won't be coming out any time soon.' His response left a sour taste in my mouth. Why? What was the difference?

'Sorry, Kenny, that's all the information I can share with you,' he replied.

Later, I would find out that the police had raided the house that morning to arrest Dami specifically. He had been under surveillance for a few months as part of a borough-wide police operation to catch drug dealers selling crack. Unbeknown to him, Dami had been selling crack cocaine and heroin to an addict who turned out to be an undercover police officer. They had an album of photographs and a playlist of voice recordings catching him in the act on multiple occasions. He was guilty as charged. So were more than a dozen other men who were raided that morning too.

When I got home that afternoon, my room looked like a tornado had hit it. While I had been in custody, the police had also decided to take a visit to my house. They didn't find anything – of course not – and they'd left as peacefully as one can in that situation. According to my mum, they had knocked politely. As they already knew I'd been taken into custody, there was no sense in booting down my door. And they didn't search the whole house, like Dayo's, they just searched my room. I had to be grateful. But it wasn't enough to spare my mum's anger.

'How could you be so irresponsible? Do you see your life?' she yelled. She'd been so shocked to see the police at our door.

'Why is that you, Kenny, of all people, have to be arrested for drugs?'

My guess was as good as hers on this one.

'I don't know, I was just sleeping at Dayo's house. I wasn't causing any trouble.'

'You should be protecting me,' she snapped back. 'Not bringing police here and drawing attention to our house.'

'I'm sorry, Mum, but I didn't do anything, I swear.' As much as I feared my mum's anger, I knew she was within her rights to feel the way she did. Mum was an immigrant, and she only had an Indefinite Leave to Remain status. This meant that although she was allowed to live and work in the UK permanently, she wasn't a British citizen. She was living on the edge – like so many other immigrants in this country. She had fought tooth and nail to get this status for herself and me and George, and she didn't want anything to jeopardize our chances of ever getting British citizenship, or worse, be deported back to Nigeria. No one had ever threatened her with this, but she must have felt the insecurity of it anyway. If I brought trouble to her door, she would be reminded of how vulnerable her legal status was. She worked hard to provide for us, but Mum didn't know about her rights or where she would stand if something happened.

That was the difference between us. She worried a lot, but for me, this was just another day in the life of a Peckham Boy. I was living on both sides of the law, and it was a life filled with crime, police troubles and at times high blood pressure. What else did I expect? I knew what I'd signed up to. I had traded my peace of mind for money, power, respect and status. Even though the last thing I wanted to do was involve my mum, I had few regrets. I'd been a broke nobody before but *look at me now*. I was a rich somebody.

But having my two lives collide, bringing my street life so close to my door, knowing what I had put my mum through, I realized this couldn't be for ever. I kept telling myself that selling weed was just a stepping stone to greater things, allowing me to indulge in a lifestyle I craved. At the same time I was also setting up a future for myself, I thought. Through my studies I was preparing myself for university and the workforce. That said, my attitude shifted as soon as I got a taste of what having a proper job actually felt like.

As Dami adjusted to life in prison during that hot summer of 2008, I was adjusting to life as a sales assistant at Dorothy Perkins. I'd started working in their flagship store in Oxford Street, in the West

End. I had never had a job before – well, not a legal one – and I was there as part of my compulsory two weeks' work experience. Everyone had to do this before starting their final year of secondary school. It would be a valuable learning experience and great for our CVs, our teachers told us. In fact, my school had arranged a placement for me in some store on the Old Kent Road, but I'd rejected it. Instead, I wanted to be in the city centre, where real business happens, so I arranged the placement with Dorothy Perkins myself. But as it turned out, I was very much out of my comfort zone, like a tropical bird in the Antarctic.

The store supervisor and team worked me hard for those two weeks. They had me running around with folded clothes and hangers for the flashy tourists to try on. Plus the bored floor staff were more than happy to dump any tasks of theirs on to me. Whatever else the experience gave me, it did give me a new-found respect for people who work in retail. Standing up all day and dealing with all types of characters who walk through the doors, all with a smile on your face, isn't easy. And doing all this hard graft for free felt like child labour. I should have been grateful for the opportunity, apparently, but I couldn't help but want something more than a generic reference at the end of my two weeks, saying how I'd turned up on time and done what was asked of me. Most days I would put in the hours, but I also made some excuses and took a couple of days off too.

The one lesson I learned – and I'm not sure it was the one my teachers had in mind – was that I didn't want to work in retail. Well, certainly not on the shop floor. It was too much work for £5 an hour. What could I do with that? I was used to making ten times that amount in a bad hour at work. No matter what way I ran the numbers, nobody working on a shop floor could make what I was making working part-time on the streets. How could I ever continue with the lifestyle I'd gotten used to on £40 a day? I would be taking a brutal pay cut to work in Dorothy Perkins, or wherever else – if I'd even wanted a proper job. I wasn't prepared to go backwards, financially, and I wasn't going to. I hadn't come this far and taken all this risk to earn a minimum wage. I was my own boss already – isn't that the dream? – so why would I give it up to be bossed around by someone a few years older, who I was already earning more than? Nah. If this was what being legit would mean for me then I was, for the time being anyway, happy to keep taking the risks.

That was my attitude for the following year or so, until the end of August edged closer. The 27th was the day I had been waiting for my entire student life. Whatever happened would determine my future options. Maybe I would be resigned to a life on the streets, or maybe a clear path would open up to me – one that I'd worked for, one that I'd earned on my own merits? Perhaps I wouldn't feel so torn? For most people, it was just another summer's day, but for me – and half a million other sixteen-year-olds – it was the day when our futures would be made or broken, the day we got our GCSE results. I had already achieved five GCSEs by the end of Year 10, a year earlier than normal, but that didn't make me any less nervous.

As soon as the sun broke through the gap in my bedroom window that the blinds didn't cover, I was wide awake. I anxiously checked the time on my BlackBerry phone, and saw I didn't have much to play with. Hurriedly, I brushed my teeth and had an African-style bucket bath – a quick wash down with soap and water scooped from a plastic bucket. My mum knew that this was a very big day for me and that I needed to get out the front door fast. However, as far as she was concerned, I still had enough time to let her pray for me, and forcibly anoint me with olive oil, a dab smeared across my forehead and scalp. Despite time ticking, I knew that of all days, today I would definitely need God's favour.

On foot as usual, I began the walk to Peckham train station, past the multiplex cinema, past the McDonald's and behind Iceland, where an immovable stench forever lingers. All the streets where danger lurked as a Peckham Boy and a drug dealer felt even more uneasy that day – the life or death of my future. Finally, when I made it to Gipsy Hill, the closest train stop to my school, a few of my friends had gathered to meet me. In the distance, I could see a swarm of people already lingering outside the school gates and I started to feel my heart beat like a Trinidadian steel pan. Underneath I may have been a bundle of nerves, but no one needed to see that. So, I raised my head and put on a strong smile to mask the tension.

As I walked past some familiar faces from my year group, I saw some of the brightest students not looking too pleased or, worse, like somebody had died. The expectation seemed all too much. And I could hear the reassuring comments of parents who had accompanied their son or daughter: 'Don't let today define your worth,' or 'Regardless of what you get, you still have a future.' I thought that as comforting as those words sounded, it was hard for this day not to mean so much to everyone, me included.

Soon, it was my turn. I headed towards reception to pick up my brown envelope. The minute I had it in my hand, I ripped it open, like a plaster on a wound. The suspense had been torturous and I needed to put myself out of my misery. As I cast my eyes down the sheet of paper, I could barely take in what I saw. Woah! In total, I'd achieved twelve GCSEs. All A–Cs. God had answered my prayers. I had smashed my exams.

Relief rushed through me, but as I took in the news I noticed other thoughts creeping in. What if I'd taken my revision and studying more seriously? All those Bs could have been As, right? And I was puzzled as to how I had retaken my maths exams from Year 10 and still got a damn C. Instead of focusing on myself and being happy with what I had achieved, I wasn't fully satisfied. In that moment I wanted more, I wanted better. Looking back, I believe that was my inner voice telling me that I really, really did want to succeed. I wasn't just playing around. I did want to study and go to university. I did want more for myself than a life on the streets. All summer I'd felt at a crossroads, but right here was my exit strategy for real.

And I knew my mum would be happy for me too. Today, she wouldn't be making her typical Nigerian parent statements like: 'I see that you got an A for this subject, but why you couldn't get an A★?' As much as these grades were a big deal for me, they were an even bigger deal for her. They would make her beam with pride, and nobody could take that away from her. These results would show that she didn't suffer the stress of raising me in vain. Also, though she never said it, these grades would earn her the bragging rights she needed to flex in conversations with my aunties and uncles.

Getting twelve GCSEs guaranteed me a place at

Richmond upon Thames College to study philosophy, politics and economics, or PPE as it's commonly known, as well as history. A lot of people in my school planned on going there too, but some of my mates didn't achieve the grades to be accepted. Instead, they would go to another college or sixth form, and others would have to retake GCSEs in their first year of college. I wondered how it had gone for the boys at the posh school next door; it was hard to imagine the same disappointment and retakes for them.

For the first time in my life, I was just delighted that I would be going to a college that I had opted for. Richmond had been my first and only choice. I couldn't wait to give up a life of wearing school uniform. I couldn't wait to go shopping and spend a lot of money on outfits. I had heard so much about how much fun Richmond College was from my older friends who were already there. Apparently, there were many girls from different areas, which was music to my ears. But, more than anything, I was ready for the challenge of studying A levels. This was the barely suppressed nerd in me talking. What normal sixteen-year-old Black boy from the hood wants to study a rich-man subject like philosophy and attempt to answer life's deepest questions?

Maybe I could start by trying to answer some of the deep questions I had about my own life.

5

You Could Become Prime Minister One Day

'If you don't do politics, then politics will do you.' –
Mike Sani, Bite The Ballot

Growing up, it felt like my mum was always watching the news on TV. I would join her sometimes. I found it interesting, whenever I could be bothered to watch. Many of the bulletins covered topics I could relate to such as poverty, unemployment, and safety on the streets, and maybe that's what gave me the ambition to study philosophy, politics, economics and history at Richmond College. But what angered me most was when I saw politicians in Parliament giving their view on subjects I felt they had no credibility to speak about. It was obvious to me that many of them didn't know how the majority lived, or understand how to bring about the equal opportunities they spoke of. How could we expect them to lift us out of poverty when almost the entire Cabinet had gone to private schools, or were raised in affluent boroughs so far removed from my own? This lot didn't know anything about our lives. How was it that they got to decide what was best for people like me? I was convinced that these politicians only understood poverty as a concept and not a reality, especially in the UK.

There were so many things that didn't make sense to me. Like why have a welfare system in our country, where sometimes you are actually better off not working than working? Or why would we have a national minimum wage that we know is too low for people like my mum to live on, even with their multiple jobs? *Why this big war on drugs,* I thought, *and not a big war on poverty?*

Even though I was about to start college, I was still surrounded by Peckham Boys like me who continued to make money selling drugs or committing other crimes. Unlike me, though, many of them thought they had no better options. Now I did have some options, but the truth was street life still had an appeal for me, even if only because I saw it as a quick way to lift me and my family out of poverty in a system that seemed set up for us to fail – and trust me, there are so many ways the system sets poor people up to fail. There were then, and there are today.

Here is just one recent example: in October 2021, the government dropped the additional £20 weekly payment that people on Universal Credit were given to help them through the Covid-19 pandemic. The benefit is given to people who don't or can't work, but also others who work in low-paid jobs and need extra help with their living costs.

Many of the people who made that decision are highly educated, privileged and extremely wealthy members of our society. It must be difficult for them to understand the importance – the lifeline – that even a small amount like £20 gives to people – people like me and my mum back then. Reducing the income of those who are already struggling by £80 a month is a big deal. How are they expected to fill the shortfall to pay for their food and bills and school uniforms for their children? Only people who have never lived in poverty, or been close enough to it, would take a move so casually. To some, £20 is just an Uber trip or the tip they add for a meal in a restaurant. But for others, it's the difference between eating and starving.

At the time of writing this book, 840,000 more people are estimated to have been moved into poverty by that one decision to drop the £20 uplift, and 290,000 of these are children.[1] Estimates also predicted that as a result of its removal, 2.3 million people would fall into debt. Now we have a cost-of-living crisis and fuel bills are rocketing. Many more will fall into debt because they don't have money in their pockets. I doubt many politicians know how people like my mum can make £20 stretch. If you budget carefully, £20 can buy food for a family, perhaps for a whole week. It can buy you pasta and fruit and vegetables, sauces and tinned food, milk and teabags, plus some meat like chicken or beef. Are you telling me that all this food doesn't make much of a difference to people's lives?

I'm sure some of those politicians also think that people who come from where I do aren't articulate enough to talk in the same way they do about the problems facing our country, but that isn't true either. While I was at school I'd started to talk about all the injustices in our society with my friends. Sure, we might not have been debating like we were at Eton or Harrow, but we still felt angry and disillusioned with politicians who made lots of promises and delivered nothing. I felt frustrated that I was repeating myself, day in, day out, while nothing around me was changing. I figured it wasn't going to be enough just to learn about politics from a textbook or what I saw on the news. I had to become a doer, not a talker. That was why a little while before my GCSE results, I joined the Labour Party.

Although it seemed an odd thing to do – and certainly not something my friends were doing – I

had already started thinking that I wanted to influence the decisions politicians made. Despite being
only fifteen, I felt this burning passion about all the
injustices that were going on around me. Perhaps
it was because I was into a life of crime that I saw
the extent that it plagued Peckham. Perhaps also,
deep down, I just wanted to find a way out. Sometimes I even thought that maybe I'd become a
Member of Parliament one day, although that
seemed like a long shot from where I was standing.
Occasionally, I pictured myself sitting on exactly
the same green leather benches in the same cham-
ber with those politicians I saw on the news, telling
them about how it really was for us, the people
their decisions affected the most.

Why Labour? All I knew was that Labour was
meant to be the best political party for Black people
and working-class people like me. Under a Labour
government I'd already benefited from having a
laptop given to each child in my secondary school
who didn't have access to one. And everyone in my
community also voted Labour, so it had been
drummed into me as a kid. My mum voted for
them religiously, and it would have been cultural
suicide to have joined the Conservatives. Everyone
said they didn't care about people like us.

When I told a few friends from school that I
had joined the Labour Party, they were happy for
me, as if it was a big deal. 'That's sick! Bruv, you

could be Prime Minister one day!' they joked. Knowing about my passion for politics, they were pleased, but also pleased I'd chosen a party known for standing up for our community. That year Obama began his presidency in the US and we'd all crammed into the school auditorium to watch his inauguration. At that moment, me and my friends saw that it was possible for someone Black to become a president. A feeling of hope rippled through us and encouraged us all to continue to dream, and wildly too.

Besides, joining a party wasn't hard to do. Anybody could apply, pay a few quid and become a member. But for me it was also a statement about investing in my future. I wanted to do something to help people in Peckham, poor people, working-class people and people facing racism. I wanted to advocate for those in society who were overlooked – people like me.

At the same time, I already knew I was part of the problem. I was still caught up in a life which involved drugs, violence, robberies and theft. I also had deep within me the fear that people who come from poverty always have: that no matter what you make of your life, you could find yourself there again. For that reason, I was scared to give up my business and leave the life I had become accustomed to. I would have to keep balancing my double life.

Even though I wanted to change things I wasn't sure what could be done about it yet. I just felt it wasn't right for people to live the way we did, or in any other area crippled by poverty and crime. I didn't *want* selling drugs to seem like the smartest option available. I didn't want to see my mum work multiple jobs just to have barely enough to get by to look after me and my brother.

However, it didn't take too long before I realized that doing politics through political parties wasn't all it was cracked up to be. I attended my first local constituency meeting one evening in a cold community hall in Camberwell, which was in desperate need of a paint job and some heating. In attendance were local councillors and other party members like me. One of the first things I noticed was that most of the people there were White, grey-haired (or no-haired) and at least three times my age – no young people other than me were in the room. I stood out like a sore thumb, even though I looked like most other people in my community. The meeting was hardly representative. The agenda was just as dull – none of the items were stimulating to me. There were updates on new street lights that had been installed and how many potholes had been fixed in the road. When one old man stood up to moan about the brightness of the lights outside his window, people's eyes rolled like they knew he was in for the long haul.

On and on he went, like he was competing in the complaining Olympics. The meeting dragged on, and my focus slipped in and out. I just wanted to speak about what we could do to change the reality of people like me, my mum, my friends and our families.

This was bureaucracy at its worst, it wasn't in any way dynamic or about campaigning. I hoped that all meetings weren't like this, so I tried one more local constituency meeting and found it as uninspiring as the first. I hadn't joined the Labour Party to be part of these types of discussion, or to bore myself silly with irrelevant conversations that didn't focus on the people I cared about. I quit the party soon after.

I wasn't even mad about it, just disappointed. I could only blame myself for believing that by simply becoming a party member I could influence what was being decided in the House of Commons. I was new to this world of politics, and I had no one to help me navigate it. But I knew in my heart that I couldn't give up. There was a voice in my head driving me on, but I just had to find a way to do things differently and carve out my own path. With the same energy I put into running my cannabis enterprise, I searched around for other ways to further my ambitions. To embark on this journey, the two things I realized I needed were experience and exposure.

I was still dealing, but by now I was also a few months into my college course, and I decided to secure some political work experience for the following summer. I wanted to be in the mix, and deepen my understanding of this unknown world. I fired off emails to a long list of MPs and politicians. Anyone I could find who seemed remotely interesting. Very few people got back to me, or even had the courtesy to acknowledge my emails at all. However, one politician did give me the time of day and offered me some work experience. Her name was Valerie Shawcross. She was a London Assembly Member for Lambeth and Southwark and had been in the role for almost a decade. She'd joined the Labour Party when she was nineteen and was now a seasoned campaigner, respected by many in the party. This was my email:

From: Kenny Imafidon
Sent: 22 Nov 2009, 23:08
To: Valerie Shawcross
Subject: could u please help
Email: I'm looking to take a path in what you are doing and especially politics . . . and i thought u could help.

In Valerie's reply she suggested I join a political party and go along to one of their local meetings. But I had already done that, I told her. I wanted more involvement with matters that affected young people and our communities. And I wasn't just interested in Peckham and Camberwell, where I lived, but the whole of London. Valerie repeated that, to do that, I would have to start at the bottom and work up. She also suggested that instead of setting my sights on becoming a politician, I might look at becoming a policy researcher, but I didn't like that idea at all. That sounded as boring as the meetings I'd sat in.

After several more email exchanges, Valerie started to realize that I wasn't taking no for an answer. I told her about my college course and that I also wanted to go on to study philosophy, politics and economics at university. After she suggested I join a political club there, I pleaded with her to give me some work experience or even just meet me to talk over a coffee – anything so I could get my foot in the door. When she immediately agreed, I was surprised.

From: Valerie Shawcross
Sent: 24 Nov 2009, 21:09
Subject RE: could u please help
Email: Hi again Kenny. Your first email didn't give me much to go on. I get a clearer picture now. Yes, I would be delighted to have a coffee and talk over whether we might find a week's work experience for you. Can you send me a

> short CV for yourself please and have a good
> look at the GLA website to brief yourself on what
> we do. I'll have a look at my diary and see when
> I might have a half hour to see you. When are
> you out of school and available? Best wishes Val.

I sent my CV across, and not long afterwards, she wrote again. Her PA would ring me and arrange time for a chat. With those words, I knew I had an 'in', and after our meeting Valerie didn't disappoint. She arranged that on the first week of my summer holidays I would shadow her at her workplace, City Hall. I'd only walked past City Hall a few times but I was fascinated by it. With its unusual shape – like an oversized headlamp – and clear glass frontage, it was unlike any building we had in Peckham, not even close. Now I would be working in it!

That day, I'd dressed in black trousers and a banker-stripe shirt and put on my smart black Ralph Lauren trainers, disguised as shoes for the job. I wasn't wearing no hard-back shoes for anyone.

'I'm here for work experience with Valerie Shawcross,' I told the receptionist after I'd made it through the airport-style security. It all seemed so formal and daunting and I felt nervous standing there in my smart clothes, knowing that the home I'd come from that morning was so different. In truth, I felt like an actor on a film set, just waiting for the guards to swoop over and drag me off at any second, like the impostor I felt I was.

'Please wait for Valerie's PA to pick you up,' the receptionist said once he'd phoned for confirmation. I was surprised I'd passed the first test of getting through automatic barriers. Now, I'd passed a second and I allowed myself to relax just a little. As I waited those few minutes in the foyer I stared up at the domed ceiling: *this is where the magic happens*, I thought. All the elected London Assembly officials are here, and the Mayor of London.

'Kenny?' Valerie's PA held out her hand to shake before leading me to the elevator which took us to her floor. Past the office entrance there were swarms of tables and meeting rooms and the floor hummed with chatter.

Suddenly, my body tensed again as questions flooded my mind. What would I say to people if they spoke to me? Would we relate to one another? What would I be asked to do? Make tea and coffee for everyone? But as I walked through the open-plan space the main question that hit me was: how would I fit in? I couldn't see anyone else who looked remotely like me.

'Just get on with it and adapt,' I kept telling myself. I smiled, held my head up and started my week.

Surprisingly, once I got started, I took it all in my stride and I felt excited by it all. My attitude was simple: if I could handle life on the streets, I could handle anything here, and I embraced every challenge and task that Valerie threw my way. I did research for her, and shadowed her in meetings. I also attended meetings that she couldn't make on her behalf, and I would take detailed notes for her so I could brief her when I saw her. I sat in on meetings where the security measures for the 2012 Olympics were being discussed, and meetings on a multimillion-pound redevelopment of Burgess Park in Southwark – my local council. I met directors, CEOs, and people of significance. Me? A Peckham Boy? This felt unreal.

One of the significant people I met was a woman called Samantha who was a director at Southwark Council and who, among other things, looked after community safety and housing in Southwark. After I attended a meeting with her and Valerie, we exchanged details, and when my week of shadowing Valerie was over I shadowed Samantha in her office, which was down the road from City Hall.

Jonathon Toy was another person I met, this time through Samantha. He was a White middle-aged man, silver-haired but very down-to-earth. He worked for Southwark Council too and was mainly involved in community safety projects. We couldn't have looked or sounded more different, but he seemed to take to me, thought I was sharp and could articulate a lot of the issues he was campaigning about from a true, lived experience. For the first time, I felt I'd met someone different to me who could empathize with our struggles. And he was very passionate about giving Peckham Boys like me a positive exit from the hood.

I never disclosed to Jonathon any of my criminal activities. I never told anyone who didn't need to know or who I couldn't trust. I even suspended my business while I did my work experience. But I realized quickly that I had some transferable skills. Just like I had grown my network selling drugs, I could grow my network in this completely new world. Every new day and every new contact I made gave me more confidence that some day soon I would be able to give up my double life for good.

From working in Samantha's office I went on to do two weeks of work experience in Harriet Harman's Parliamentary office, while she was Acting Leader of the Opposition. That one foot in the door with Valerie Shawcross had opened up a whole series of opportunities I could only have dreamed of. Valerie and Harriet were good friends, and Harriet was the Labour MP for Camberwell and Peckham – the MP my mum helped to vote in at every single general election. I didn't get to meet Harriet herself, but I was thrilled to be working inside the world-famous Houses of Parliament, the so-called mother of all parliaments.

The morning I was to start, I took the number

12 bus from Peckham all the way there. Nervous I
would be late, or get lost, I had left the house very
early. I'd only ever been to Parliament once before,
on a college trip when we'd toured the House of
Commons and the Lords, but when it came to actually working there, I had no idea what to expect.

Harriet's office was in Portcullis House, directly
opposite Big Ben. The first thing I noticed were
the armed officers, clasping their sub-machine guns,
with itchy trigger fingers ready to shoot instantly
at any deadly threats. Their presence would make
anyone have second thoughts about doing anything stupid here, I thought. I watched them
intently as I waited for Harriet's assistant, Daniel,
to pick me up from reception.

'Hi, Kenny, let me show you around,' he
offered, giving me a quick tour of Portcullis House
before we reached the office. On the way, he
pointed out where I could buy a subsidized lunch,
and the bustling public spaces and personal offices
for MPs. By now, any nerves I'd had – similar to
those I felt at City Hall – had disappeared. I felt
like I was at a theme park, enjoying every ride,
curious to see what was round every corner and
where the journey would take me.

And just like at City Hall, I put on a good act,
changing my manner immediately when I was
introduced to the three-person team I would be
working with. Handshakes and how-do-you-dos.

Pleased to meet you. Never words I would use on the street where 'Yo, Bruv' and 'Wagwan' would be my everyday greeting. But I knew I couldn't bring my street self to the workplace. I have to code-switch, as it's known. I couldn't risk being seen as 'hood' or be treated as 'less than' because I didn't adapt to my environment. I even switched up the language I used in emails: *Hope you are doing well, Kind Regards* and *Yours Sincerely* – words that would be laughed at if I used them in Peckham, but I had to blend in here by any means.

If truth be told, the thought that I would be working in Parliament turned out to be more exciting than the actual experience itself. The building was quieter than usual because it was summer recess. There were no lively Prime Minister's Questions. No Parliamentary debates. No committee sessions. All I could do was manage the case work I was assigned.

Soon, I began to grasp the sheer amount of case work that an MP has to deal with. People contact MPs about everything from housing problems to immigration issues to a problem with their central heating boiler at home. At the time, the war in Iraq was ongoing so there were also many letters from constituents complaining that the allied invasion was illegal.

My job was not to solve everyone's problem. Instead, I had to ask more questions, take notes, and put them in touch with relevant agencies and organizations who would act on their behalf or provide them with necessary information. It wasn't glamorous, but it was educational, and a privilege. At the end of a busy two weeks I felt I'd achieved another important milestone – unlike my secondary school work experience at Dorothy Perkins, where all I achieved was organizing piles of women's clothes in order of size on a rack. I had to remind myself how far I'd come. Now, I had experience working in the offices of local, regional and national political figures. Based on the summer's experience my personal statement for my UCAS form, which would help get me to university, was going to look just like those submitted by the kids at the private college next door to my old school. But there would be one big difference: I'd made it happen myself; no one had done it for me. No mummy or daddy's contacts involved. I was seizing every opportunity I could to learn more about politics and the day-to-day lives of decision makers. I was building connections in a world totally foreign to my own.

Back on my home turf, though, I was still walking a tightrope. I'd tasted sweet opportunities through my work experience, and I knew in my head and heart that I had to continue chasing my dreams. I didn't want to be one of those guys in their thirties still selling drugs, going through a revolving door of prison and parole, but it wasn't always that easy to leave that life behind. Whenever I thought about giving it up, my savings would get low and suddenly all of my good intentions got shoved to the back of my mind. Besides, all of my friends were still in Peckham and the same life carried on.

And it seemed like a wave of violence was erupting, becoming more serious by the day. Stabbings were already commonplace, but now shootings felt as regular as the sound of ice cream vans in the summer. People had tried to shoot at me too, but so far, they'd missed.

One particular night is as clear to me now as if it was a scene from a film. I'd just left Dayo's house with my friend Ola. It was near midnight and we were minding our own business, chatting and laughing as usual. I was looking forward to getting to bed after a long night of gaming and catching up.

But just as we were walking, a *BANG* punctured the night air. What the hell? Heart racing, I looked up, frantically searching for any colours that might be lighting up the sky. But I knew that sound. This was no firework. This was a gun.

Instantly, I turned to see where the shot had come from. In the darkness, I vaguely recognized the face of the shooter now walking brazenly towards us. He was a guy who'd fallen out with one of our friends. He'd been shot at himself earlier that day, and this was revenge. With the blood pumping in our veins, we legged it down the road out of the shooter's sight. Pausing to catch my breath, I turned to Ola. 'This guy must be out of his mind! Is he dumb?' I panted. 'Watch when we catch him . . .' This is the hood, a constant cycle of tit-for-tat. I'd done nothing to that shooter directly, but I was a close shave away from a bullet. As we ran from the scene, my mind turned to revenge. I didn't start anything, but now I could be forced to finish it.

In the end, I didn't have to. An older Peckham Boy intervened and I got an apology. 'The guy thought you was someone else,' I was told. I still wanted revenge, and I was prepared to get it, but after that incident I never saw him again – fate stepped in, and it was probably for the best.

As I started my second year back at college and resumed my drugs business, I felt even more conflicted. Sometimes I could see light at the end of the tunnel. At other times, I was so confused. I didn't know where I stood or what my future could hold. Some days, you could find me carrying my backpack home from college, but it would be anybody's guess whether I had a hundred grams of weed in there or just my philosophy and history books.

Then, one day I got a phone call. 'Hi, Kenny. I have something to ask you . . .' I recognized the voice immediately. It was Jonathon Toy, the man I had done work experience with the previous summer. Since then, Jonathon and I had continued to be in touch, and he'd taken me under his wing. He'd brought me to some meetings and events and had given me a platform to share my insights and experiences.

Jonathon was becoming an increasingly influential figure in the community safety and youth violence space, and with the latest report he'd written, he had moved on from community politics. Now, he had the ear of government.

'Kenny, would you like to speak at an event that's being held at the Home Office?' he asked. I couldn't believe it. Me? Speaking to important officials in government? This man was something else, and I glowed with pride at the opportunity. Looking back now, Jonathon was showing me the value of my talents and my lived experience. He was the first person in politics to pay me for my time, and his support was priceless.

Jonathon's report was all about how to reduce youth violence and knife crime in communities like Peckham, and for the event he wanted us to do a joint presentation. 'Don't worry, the people we'll be talking to will just be some Home Office officials,' he said. Immediately, that made me feel more at ease. These were people I'd done work experience alongside, I told myself. It's not like I was speaking in front of an important minister. On the day, I felt confident walking through the doors of the Home Office beside Jonathon, even though I'd never been there before.

In the room, chairs had been laid out around a huge round table. It wasn't long before guests started arriving, and it was only then that I realized that these weren't just 'Home Office officials'. I would be presenting to the Home Secretary, Theresa May. Jonathon confessed he hadn't told me in case I got too worried.

Fortunately, by the time it sunk in what a big deal this actually was, the adrenaline was pumping and I just went with the moment. I listened as Jonathon introduced his report and highlighted the key points which flashed up on a big screen behind us. Then, he gave me the floor.

I took a deep breath and started talking. I hadn't even prepared a script. I spoke off the cuff like a freestyle rapper, and from the heart about the challenges facing young people from areas like mine, and the importance of having valuable, consistent and trustworthy services to help us. I spoke about how key services had to work together, to support young people, particularly those who wanted to exit a violent and criminal lifestyle.

It was so silent that you could hear a pin drop. When I looked around the room, I could see how people were listening intently to what I had to say. I was no Obama, but my speech had captivated them. Afterwards, I had to remind myself that I was just a teenager, and I'd had the attention of one of the country's most senior politicians. And when I'd looked at Theresa May's face, she was nodding and genuinely taking in my words.

When I got home that evening, I reflected on the day. I felt so grateful for the opportunity to represent the voices and realities faced by people in the hood. The humble pride I felt doing this was unlike anything I had felt before. Selling weed for a living was easy and almost anybody could do it – but this work was different.

I could look around me and blame the government. I could blame Peckham or I could blame my dad for some of the choices I had made. It's easy to find someone or something else to blame, but that wouldn't make a difference to my actual circumstances. I knew I had to take responsibility for my situation – was it time now to give up my drug-selling for good? I started to think about other people from Peckham who had been dealt the same cards in life, or an even worse hand, and who had made different choices. There were celebrities like the footballer Rio Ferdinand who'd come from an estate not far from me. He'd lifted himself out of poverty with hard work and skill. But there were also people I knew of who weren't famous: people who'd simply decided enough was enough and moved to another part of London to lead a quiet life. I knew it would soon be time to make my choice.

6

The Last Dance

*'Live In The Moment . . . Dance like it's your last
dance . . . Sing like it's your last song . . . Laugh like
it's your last laugh . . . And love like it's your last
romance . . . Everyone isn't given a second chance so
seize the moment.'* – Theresa Lewis

By December 2010 it had been around four months
since my internship with Valerie, and I'd also continued to work off and on with Jonathon. While I
felt satisfied that I had some political connections,
I still came home to the same community struggling to play the cards life had dealt it. Sure, I could
pause my business when doing work experience at
City Hall, or when I needed to work with Jonathon on something important, like a talk with
professionals or a presentation. For those hours or
days or weeks I became an upstanding citizen, but

as soon as the work ended, I was back to selling weed. At heart, I was still a Peckham Boy, looking over my shoulder, making money the way I always had. I was just seventeen years old. A kid. I hoped that somehow, sometime soon things would change, but it felt like change wasn't happening fast enough. I wanted to go to university, and one more thing spurring me on was that tuition fees were going to be tripled for students, from £3,000 a year to as much as £9,000 for those who were starting in 2012. It felt like my time to get on was running out. When the new year rolled around, I vowed that the next year would be different. 2011 would be the year things changed for good.

In that no man's land after Christmas, when the days seem short and aimless, I was bored and restless, itching for something to do. I ended up going to Sodiq and Qudus's house. Sodiq was a friend I'd known for five years. He was in the year above me at school and we'd met each other when I joined Peckham Youngsters Football Club. He played on the right wing, and I played right back. We were a real duo on the pitch, him speeding down the wing, skilfully swerving the threat of a defender with a one-two pass, while I legged it over to receive the ball. Together, we set up so many winning goals. Over time our relationship extended beyond the football pitch and being just teammates – we became brothers.

Qudus, his brother, was my age, and though we got along well I wasn't as close to him as Sodiq. I didn't have deep chats with him in the same way, and I didn't know what the future looked like for him. Though they were brothers with just one year separating them, they looked nothing alike. Just like my brother George, Qudus was darker in complexion, and they clashed in the way George and I often did.

The brothers lived in a notorious north Peckham estate. Like me also, they were from a Nigerian background and, along with their little sister, were being raised in a single-parent family by their healthcare-worker mum. When people had nowhere else pressing to be, their house became a sort of hub in the community. Even at ungodly hours of the night, friends were always welcome, unless their mum wanted us out.

'You got good grades, bro, you can do a course!' I'd told Sodiq that evening. He also had big dreams to get out of the hood. He'd got good GCSE results but hadn't gone on to college. I was always trying to persuade him to go back to his studies. 'We'll both be doing something with our lives!' I laughed, before giving him a rundown of everything I was doing to further my political dreams. In between, we played *Call of Duty: Black Ops*, the newest game on Xbox at the time, and caught up on the latest hood gossip.

Whatever the year held for us, it was going to be a year of change. I was due to turn eighteen, and Sodiq's childhood sweetheart had just had a baby so he'd recently become a dad. As we talked and played computer games, the hours tumbled on and I ended up sleeping over. I was still at his the next afternoon, with not much to do but chill.

Then, I picked up my phone. I noticed I had a missed call from my uncle. 'George is sick,' he said when I called him back. 'You should take him to the GP.' Apparently, George had developed a fever and a strange rash had started appearing across his body, which was odd because when I'd seen him the day before he'd seemed all right, and had been making plans to see his friends. He seemed a bit under the weather, but nothing serious.

'When you've done that, you should go home and clean up the house,' my uncle continued rudely. My mum had spent the holidays in Nigeria and would be back that day. He knew, and I knew, how mad she would be if she returned to see the house in a mess, or with the lights still on – she would go crazy.

'Okay, okay,' I grumbled. I was having fun at Sodiq's and dragged my feet. The last thing I wanted to do was waste hours in a GP's waiting room, when I could be here instead. Besides, the GP's was only round the corner, so I came up with a plan. If my brother could get himself there on his own, I could meet him there a little later.

I arrived at the GP surgery half an hour later only to find that George hadn't made it yet, and after many BBM messages between us I headed home. He was at his friend Sebastian's house, he said, and he was leaving soon. Eventually, George messaged to tell me he'd made it to the GP but there was a queue and he would meet me back at Mum's.

For the rest of that afternoon I sorted out the house, making sure it looked like how my mum left it. But I was worrying about George and whatever was wrong with him. *Mum will know how best to look after George*, I thought. *Best wait for her.* And I was right. As soon as her bags landed in the hallway, she was on mum-duty and giving him tablets and water. She reckoned he had chickenpox, which he did, and she promised to take him to the GP herself the next morning. She was angry that he didn't wait in the queue – or maybe that I didn't wait with him.

That evening, I settled in the living room while Mum took up her usual spot on the sofa to watch a film. Suddenly, my phone started blowing up.

There are bare feds round my bit, and I see they've taped off some block. You know what happened? I heard one guy got hit up, a friend had written. I had been completely oblivious, just chilling out.

Nah you know bro, I messaged back.

But I didn't have to look far to find out more. It took just seconds of scrolling through BB Messenger to see the updated statuses: emojis with crying faces and angel emojis. Another status read: *I think somebody died on ends.*

Died? I kept scrolling.

Then Nicola, a friend from college, messaged me: *You heard anything about Sylvester? Is he dead?*

He can't be dead, I thought.

Sylvester Akapalara was a 17-year-old who was in the year below me at college. He wasn't a close friend, but we had mutual friends, both from college and from Peckham. Whenever we bumped into each other it was always good vibes. I would always banter him too. I thought he was cool. I sat back down, thoughts racing. Sylvester? Dead? It was unnerving even if it was someone you didn't know, but this guy was a friend. I was really hoping this was not true.

Then, a phone call from another college friend who was very close to him: 'Is it true? Is Sylvester dead? I think he is, you know, because apparently he ain't answering his phone.'

It was true. Sylvester was dead. A talented athlete, full of potential, who could have been in the Olympics one day, had been murdered, gunned down in a stairwell in a block of flats in the nearby Pelican Estate. In any other place, you would have thought a death like that would be shocking, and it was, but in Peckham it had also become part of everyday life. Here, there were more knives than in a busy restaurant; more shootings than in a western. And nine times out of ten it was young Black men who were dying.

Even in that past year the body count had been sobering. In June, a 17-year-old boy from Peckham, Samuel Ogunro, had been savagely killed. Shot in the back of the head, with his body left to burn in a blazing car. In my whole life in Peckham, I had never heard of such a brutal killing. An execution.

And not long after Sylvester's killing, an 18-year-old, who had gone to my secondary school, had died. Daniel Graham was stabbed twenty-four times in a vicious attack after he got off a bus following a party that up to a hundred young people had attended.

With all this death looming in the air, I knew more than ever that me and my friends had to be vigilant. There were enemies on all sides. Our instinct was never to be cowed into hiding. We had too much pride, and far too little common sense and respect for the consequences of our actions – but occasionally, when the heat got turned up, we knew to disappear, if only for a short while.

For this reason, not long after 2011 ushered itself in, I moved to Islington. By then, I'd hoped to have made far more steps into real politics, but instead I was neck-deep in the politics of the street — far more than I could have ever imagined. I hid things from my mum as best I could, but she wasn't stupid. She knew exactly what Peckham was like, and how dangerous it was for boys like me.

When I left I took George with me to a flat a stone's throw away from Regent's Canal. Mum would be safe where she was on her own — and safer without me there. There was no way I wanted either of them to be collateral damage in a war that had nothing to do with them. Besides, having death come so close to me on several occasions, I knew more than most how precious it was to reach adulthood. For a while anyway, George would have to travel the long distance across London each morning and evening to attend his secondary school, but it was worth it so he didn't get caught up in the violence of the hood. He was already getting drawn into the lifestyle and I was determined to drag him out of it.

If a week is a long time in politics, on the streets it's even longer. We had only been away for a few weeks, but during this time several people I knew from the hood had been arrested for various murders and crimes. One week your friends are there and the next they're gone.

By April 2011, spring was in full swing, and even though I was a good ten miles away, I still had my ear to what was happening. Now, a few of my own friends had been arrested for Sylvester's murder. Sodiq and Qudus had both been arrested and questioned. Another friend called David had been taken in too, and then Jordan. They all had been put on remand in prison and were awaiting trial. When I thought about it, most of the people I was close to were now behind bars.

One afternoon I was sat on the sofa, phone glued to my cheek. The person I was talking to was Afua, a girl from Peckham I used to chill with. We were catching up, and hearing her voice felt like the warmest thing in that room. I'd come from Peckham with few belongings. The flat was cold – just the bare essentials around me and nothing like my mum's house, piled high with suitcases. I didn't even *have* a suitcase. I'd just brought our belongings in those sturdy plastic, chequered laundry bags every Nigerian owns – so-called Ghana-Must-Go bags – and they were scattered about the floor.

Suddenly, I heard a knock at the door. 'Hold on, Afua,' I told her, pulling myself up. I had no clue who it was. No one knew I was here. Could it be a neighbour? Maybe some annoying salesperson? I looked through the spyhole. One grown White guy stood outside in casual clothes looking serious. I didn't recognize him, so reckoned I could get rid of him quickly.

Afua was still on the line when I opened the

door, but there wasn't just one man now. Several filed into view, who'd been waiting, hidden, near the door. 'Kenny Imafidon?' the main guy said. I realized this was no social visit. I quickly locked off Afua who was still on the phone, frowning at the guy now eyeballing me.

'Kenny Imafidon. We're arresting you for the murder of . . .' Those were the only words I heard. As he and the others pushed their way through the door, I felt the tops of my legs almost give way, one word ringing in my ears. Murder.

'Murder? What murder?' I asked. But as the plain-clothed officer started reading out my rights, I tuned out completely. It was just noise. In what felt like slow motion I watched as the other officers scoured the room, snatching my laptop off the sofa. I'd been writing an essay for college before Afua called. Other devices, like my phones, got snatched too. And some of my clothes got taken. Then, I was handcuffed and led outside to a waiting vehicle.

As the unmarked police car weaved its way through the traffic, I sat speechless on the back seat. I was racking my brain to understand what murder I was being arrested and questioned for. As far as I was concerned, I didn't kill anybody.

When we arrived at Islington Police Station, I already knew the drill. I could call a duty solicitor and I'd be put in a cell until that person arrived.

That day, it turned out to be Mohammed Zeb – an intelligent and no-nonsense British Pakistani. 'They have arrested you for the murder of Sylvester Akapalara,' he told me in our private pre-interview conversation. Sodiq, Qudus, David, Jordan and now me. *The police must be desperate to stick this on anyone*, I thought. 'You don't need to answer any of the questions put to you. You should stick to saying "no comment",' he said, in his thick Birmingham accent. I knew that drill too.

You would have thought that with me saying nothing, the interview time would have flown by, but it didn't. All afternoon, the questions kept coming.

'Are you friends with Sodiq?'

'No comment.'

'Did you meet with Sodiq on 29 December?'

'No comment.'

'What were you doing on that night?'

'No comment.'

On and on it went. The supposedly quick-fire interrogation took so long that they had to pause the interview for a number of breaks. The officers tried to play friendly, but it was obvious to me that they thought I was guilty. I'd been brought up to believe that the police were not our friends, and nobody could tell me any different. It was easy enough for me to work out that the questions being asked were aimed at proving my guilt rather than my innocence. Even the ones that sounded as if they might help me prove my innocence couldn't be trusted – thrown out as bait. If I wasn't careful I could end up hanging myself with the same rope being dangled in front of me.

Exhausted and frustrated, I was relieved when the officers finally pressed stop on the tape. That day, I was released on bail. No evidence to charge me. I thanked Mohammed Zeb for his help. I had hoped a very good solicitor would represent me, but when the state pays for your legal help, beggars can't be choosers. It was a game of Russian roulette but thankfully Mohammed Zeb was as good as I'd hoped and he'd secured my freedom, for now at least.

The questioning had been scary, but it was also confusing. For days afterwards, I ran through the events in my head. I tried to work back from the messages that had started flashing up on my phone when I was home with Mum and George on the day of Sylvester's murder.

I knew I'd been at Sodiq's the night before, and left his some time in the afternoon ... Then, it clicked. That was the day George was sick. The day he was supposed to meet me at the GP's but never showed. The day he got chickenpox. We were messaging each other that afternoon, so there would be evidence, right? And this was the day my mum came back from Nigeria and met me at home.

Surely she was a reliable witness? I vaguely remembered, too, that on the way back from the GP's I'd met Sodiq, who had been in Peckham to grab some food. He'd walked me home to pick up a spare phone and left not long after.

My bail conditions meant that I had to return to the same police station in a few weeks' time. It was hard to put that out of my mind, but I tried to forget. Every day, I hoped that something would happen and the whole situation would just disappear.

When Saturday, 7 May rolled around, I finally had some respite from the anguish. On that day, I turned the big 1-8. Somehow, it felt like I'd made it to this age, against the odds. I made sure I celebrated, too. Friends of mine, triplets Toni, Tosin and Toyin shared my birthday and they had done all the hard work of organizing a party. I came to celebrate with them but, cheekily, also took the opportunity to invite some of my friends from Peckham, including a few guys who the triplets understandably weren't fond of. These were friends who had a reputation of turning up and crashing parties, particularly if they weren't welcomed with open arms. So, in the run-up to that night I carried out more diplomacy than the UN: sweet-talking the triplets with promises that none of my friends would cause any trouble. After all, it was a special night for them, but it was a special night for me too, and I didn't want anyone to ruin it. Of all the days my friends needed to be on their best behaviour, this was one of them.

The party itself was taking place in a sweatbox of a bar in Waterloo. Turning eighteen meant that I could have a great time legally, for once. No sending friends who looked older to the bar. Dry ice smoke hung in the air. Gold chains sparkled and trainers shone on the dance floor. I dressed for the occasion: a brilliant white Ralph Lauren sleeve top and a mini high-top Afro haircut – hard to not feel confident. And the women-to-men ratio was looking pretty good, too. One girl, Jasmine – tall, caramel-skinned with an eye-grabbing body – was someone I loved to chat with but I always knew she wanted more from me than I could give. Nevertheless, the DJ nudged us together with his tunes, speakers blasting out my favourite Afrobeats and bashment songs while we swung our hips and locked our waists together.

And once the sounds of Bobby Valentino started to play I knew the vibe was mellowing and we'd be grinding on the dance floor to back-to-back slow jams.

It was the early hours of the morning when we spilled out on to the pavement. Nobody was in a rush to head home. Instead, we hung outside the venue, chatting loudly, making noise with no respect for the neighbours. As far as we were concerned, we owned the streets. As for me, I was waved on Courvoisier, Grey Goose and tequila shots. I had been downing alcohol all night like it was water. Now I was just aware enough to watch some guys making moves on women, some clearly with no success.

Once I was home I lay in bed. Bleary-eyed and with my head still spinning, I scrolled through my phone at the many messages that kept landing. *Happy Birthday Bro!* some said, while others recounted what a great night it had been. Love and appreciation washed over me, but moments later a darkness started to descend.

However hard I tried, no partying or alcohol was going to take away this sudden feeling of utter emptiness. All evening I'd been trying to kid myself that everything was good. But the truth was it was far from good. As the sun came up I was struggling to stay in the moment and embrace my special birthday high. Back in the real world I was still on bail and due to return to the police station.

My phone rang. It was one of my friends, Riah. 'Happy birthday, Kenny,' she said, filled with excitement and happiness.

'Thank you, Riah,' I replied with a fake energy.

'What's wrong with you? Why do you sound so low, it's your birthday!' She had clearly sussed my big act out.

'Everything is calm, you know, trust me, I'm

just tired,' I replied, trying again to sound convincing.

'Umm hmm.'

I was only fooling myself. She was right. I was
low, in a hole. I wished I could have told her the
truth about my situation, and that I was terrified
that I could go to jail on the coming Monday, put
on remand like my other friends. But either my
pride – or more likely my shame – couldn't let me
open up, so I carried on with the lie. I sat up in bed
and injected real energy into my voice. 'For real,
Riah, I am blessed. Thank you for calling, yeah. I
appreciate it and we'll speak soon.'

I promised I would call her back in a couple of
hours. But I never did.

7

Looking at a Thirty-Year Sentence

'Never be a prisoner of your past, it was just a lesson not a life sentence.' – Anonymous

Two days later, with my head feeling heavy, I made my way to Islington Police Station. The feeling was more nerve-racking than any other time I'd stepped inside a police station. This time, I could feel my skin prickle and my stomach clench. I had no idea what to expect. I knew that officers wanted to question me again, and I'd been told that I would also take part in an identity parade. I'd be lined up with others who looked like me, so an eyewitness could pick one of us out, if they recognized a person.

Although I'd been brought in by the police a handful of times before, I knew I was fortunate enough not to have a criminal record, and I had never been to prison, unlike many of my friends. I hoped my luck would continue – though I also knew that my drug-dealing and money-making enterprises weren't doing me any favours.

Before I'd even left the house, Mum wanted to pray for me, like she had done countless times before. I thought it was funny that even the biggest of criminals who live lawlessly, all come to know God in times of trouble and seek Him diligently in moments of need. Until then, I'd never quite understood why that was the case, but I'd seen it often enough – the longing, the looking to the skies, the clasped hands. I'd heard my mum tell me she was praying for me all the time, but I'd never really spoken to God myself. But here I was, another hypocrite and selfish prodigal son, seeking God's help now, in my time of trouble. I prayed He was listening.

I kept telling myself that everything would be fine but at times the anxiety gripped me. Hopefully, I would not be picked out of a line-up and the police would realize they had made a mistake. I was not a murderer. They would realize I did not kill Sylvester and 'no further action' would be taken. The case would be dropped and I could be free from all this stress. At the very least, my bail would be extended if they needed to carry out more inquiries. If there was one thing God gave, it was hope.

When I arrived, I could see my solicitor Mohammed Zeb waiting for me. From the reception desk
I was taken through to another part of the station,
which housed the custody suite. There, Mohammed reaffirmed that I'd face further questioning
but that the identification parade would come
first. I'd only ever seen this in movies before, and I
pictured myself in a dark room staring ahead with
others who looked more or less like me. *No one will
pick me out*, I thought. *How could they?* We sat in the
waiting room while everything was prepared.
Then, I turned to see one of the officers in charge
of the case walk towards us.

'Can I please have a word with you, Mr Zeb?'
he said. He took Mohammed to one side. He spoke
quietly so I couldn't quite hear his conversation.
Plus his back was turned so I couldn't lip-read
either. I strained my ears. Still nothing, other than
one sentence which would change the course of
my life for ever.

'We are going to charge him.'

Maybe I'd misheard? Charge me? For Sylvester's murder? This can't be right! No way! At that
moment, my heart dropped to my feet.

When Mohammed came back over he confirmed my fears. Very calmly, he told me the
Crown Prosecution Service had granted the police
permission to charge me. Blood was pounding
around my head. Everything Mohammed was

telling me was going in one ear and straight out of the other. I couldn't make sense of it. This couldn't be happening to me. Why would God allow this to happen to me? Also, I wasn't only being charged with murder. When the list was read out it seemed never-ending.

One count of murder
Two counts of attempted murder
Two counts of grievous bodily harm
Possession of a firearm
Possession of an offensive weapon

The superintendent reeled it off like he was ordering food in a restaurant. Then he said that the list of offences I was being charged with was under a law called joint enterprise.

At the time I'd never heard the words before, but it didn't take me long to understand. Joint enterprise is a legal doctrine created over three hundred years ago. It was initially designed to combat illegal duelling between aristocrats. The surviving duellist who had killed his opponent could be convicted but also anyone else who aided, supported, or encouraged the duel. Everyone could be jointly charged with murder. Around 2009, this doctrine had been taken from the shelves, dusted off, and revitalized in an effort to tackle gang-related violence, particularly homicides in London, which had reached a record level among teens like me.

The legal principle is that if one or more

'primary offenders' commit a murder, but other 'secondary offenders' intended to encourage or assist them to do it, then they can be prosecuted as if they'd committed the actual crime. A secondary defendant can be found guilty without even having an intent to kill or commit serious harm. They simply just have to foresee that their co-defendant 'might' kill, or 'might' inflict serious harm.

In my case, the joint enterprise, as far as I could wrap my head around it, was this: the prosecution believed that Sodiq, Qudus and I, as well as Jordan and David, all had a role to play in Sylvester's murder, whether as 'primary' or 'secondary' offenders. Later I learned that the prosecution's evidence against me was data from my mobile phone – so-called cell-site evidence – which put me in the vicinity of the scene of the crime at the time of murder, even though it couldn't prove what exact location. It also picked up that I'd been in communication with some of the others that day. I'd been at Sodiq's place, after all. But I *lived* in Peckham. And we were friends. And I also hung out near the area where Sylvester's murder took place, which also wasn't too far from my own home. Surely, cell-site evidence alone couldn't be enough to send me to prison?

The expression 'seeing your life flash before your eyes' suddenly made a lot of sense. I had turned eighteen two days ago; this was not the birthday present I'd been hoping for. I was staring straight down the barrel of a minimum thirty-year prison sentence. If found guilty, I would be in prison until 2041. I wouldn't be going to Malia this summer, as planned, or to university in the autumn. I wouldn't be going anywhere for thirty years.

One minute, I'd been giving presentations to the likes of Home Secretary Theresa May – I'd been doing my best to build a different life for myself – and the next I was here. While I wasn't a saint, by any means, I wasn't a murderer. My head was in tatters as I stared up at the ceiling of the custody suite and read words that had been painted across it . . . *Are you sick and tired of feeling sick and tired?* Underneath them was a helpline number. Trapped in this room, I was certainly sick and tired of reading and rereading those words.

Mohammed ran through what would happen next. I would appear in court first thing the next morning and it was very likely I would be remanded in custody. If I pleaded guilty then the case would move quickly and I would be sentenced. If I pleaded not guilty, as we were both sure I would, there would be a trial. Like my friends, my fate would be in the hands of twelve jurors who may, or may not, believe my story.

As I sat, trying to make sense of what had happened, I recognized the feeling at the core of it all. Shame.

I felt it for myself but, more than anything, I felt it for my mum.

Mummy's golden boy was going to be in prison.

I should have been her first child to earn an internationally recognized degree from a top-ranking, world-class university. But instead, I was going to be the first of her children to earn the title of prisoner. What would my mother and my family think of me now? What would the gossips back home and in the church say about her? Would people say she had failed me as a mother because of where I'd ended up?

Mixed in with that shame was a strong dose of anger. More than ever, I was pissed off at the police. How could they use me like this as a pawn in their investigation? All they'd done was make themselves look as though they were doing a great job by arresting various suspects, no matter how weak the evidence against them. I would be framed as a potential killer, even though I was – in theory at least – innocent until proven guilty.

Then, another thought swallowed me up. My name would be all over the newspapers and TV news reports – those same bulletins that had inspired me to get into politics. My name would be heard by people who respected me, who liked me, who loved me, yet now they would think of me as a killer. Would they think I was capable of that, or would they stand by me and believe my story?

What would all those friends who rang me on the night of Sylvester's murder think of me now? Would they believe that I lied? Would they believe that I ambushed Sylvester and I pulled the trigger that killed him on the stairs? Who would believe I'd done it, and who would believe I hadn't? How many of our mutual friends would be asking, shocked, what kind of guy was I if I was capable of murder, in cold blood and in broad daylight, of someone who I had laughed and joked with, and who had done me no wrong?

I was charged in the middle of the afternoon and told I would have to spend the night in the police cell. When I finally had the chance to make my one legal phone call, I spoke to my mum. Disappointment and shame were in my voice, though I did my best to sound brave and to let her know that I was all right. I told her I was going to court tomorrow. And, based on what Mohammed told me, that I was very likely going to prison too.

'You just be prayerful, Kenny, the Lord is not sleeping,' Mum told me.

From where I was standing, I couldn't see how God was awake or with me.

I still replied, 'I will, Mum,' even though I knew I would struggle to pray. Yet I knew that was what she would want to hear from me right now.

'What time will you be going to court? Please

let me know so that I can be there,' she asked caringly.

'I'm not too sure, Mum, but Mohammed will be in touch and let you know all the details.'

With the officer signalling to me to wrap up my phone call, I quickly steered the conversation to a close. 'I have to go, Mum. I will try and call you again later, but if not I will see you tomorrow.' Mum shed no tears, but I could hear both sadness and hope in her voice. Although I had just told her that I had to go, in her typical Nigerian fashion, she thought it was still a good time to share a short prayer with me – at least her version of a short prayer, which was a minute too long for the impatient officer, now frowning and wildly circling his hand. She would be in court the next day to support me, she said, before the line went dead. After everything I'd put her through, I couldn't have asked for more.

That night, I tried to sleep but I couldn't find any peace. The bed wasn't helping either. This was no Silentnight mattress. How did they expect me to rest or sleep comfortably on this blue padded mat? The type you use to exercise on in school PE lessons. I looked around the greyish-looking walls and at the tiny silver toilet and sink, then up at the ceiling that was so high for the purpose of stopping anyone who might try to commit suicide. To pass the time, I read some of the magazines that had been left lying around. One was a Chelsea FC magazine from a few years ago, but time still dragged even without a clock in my police cell. At one stage, I even resorted to counting the bricks on the cell walls. Nothing worked.

I was to be taken to Camberwell Green Magistrates' Court. This was a court I knew well, as I had appeared as a defendant there once before. That time it had been for the minor offence of obstructing a police officer. I'd refused to let him stop and search me by the bus stop at Camberwell Green.

I hated being stopped and searched – and had lost count of how many times it had happened before. Under Section 60 rules, a police officer can stop and search us without suspicion or any reasonable grounds. But Section 60 was abused, I am sure. I was convinced they were stopping a lot of me and my Black friends because, to put it simply, we were Black. The statistics tell a disturbing story too. The latest figures show that young Black men are twenty-nine times more likely to be searched for weapons than the population at large.[1] What is also most annoying for me is that 76 per cent of all stop and searches result in no further action.[2] That said, I had actually been okay with it on that occasion. I knew the police had a job to do and they weren't always picking solely on me. The problem was that these officers wanted to do it in a very public place.

'Can we go somewhere more private?' I had asked them, quite politely. But for that particular officer my request was too much of an ask. So, my ignorant and stubborn self resisted, and I got arrested. I was charged with obstructing a police officer, but when I later appeared in court the judge dismissed the case. Thankfully, he knew it was a waste of time and that I was a good kid anyway – at least to the naked eye.

Today, though, was way more serious, and I felt the weight of it on me. I knew that my solicitor would try to get me bail, but the reality was that he had a better chance of breaking me out of my handcuffs and smuggling me from the court, than persuading the judge of my innocence. And, when it came to it, the judge wasn't swayed by any of Mohammed's arguments. There was no concrete evidence against me that should have led to me being charged: my blood had not been found at the scene. No one had identified or mentioned my name as a possible suspect. I had not been spotted on CCTV. Operation Trident, a police unit set up to tackle gun murders in Black communities, had only circumstantial evidence against me. This was the mobile phone evidence showing communication between me and another suspect – who I spoke to on a daily basis – but the issue here was that I'd done so around the time of the murder.

Mohammed pleaded with the judge that the evidence was weak. So what if I'd been in contact with another suspect? That didn't make me guilty of murder and certainly not enough grounds to charge someone and potentially expose them to a life sentence. However, the prosecution argued, and the judge agreed, that I would be a threat to witnesses if I was allowed to run free. He said I was likely to intimidate them and this might taint their evidence, or it might stop people from coming forward at all. It was now Tuesday 11 May and I was to be remanded until 9 November. Six months. As the judge spoke those words, my stomach almost caved in.

Six months? In my head I was screaming and swearing at the judge and the prosecution, but outwardly I just stared ahead, my mouth getting drier and my body tensing further. I was going to jail. My luck all these years of dodging prison had come to an end. I was meant to be the lucky one, who never ever went inside. Well, now I was the very unlucky one, looking at a lifetime in prison for a murder I did not commit.

I looked at him, as if to appeal, but the judge's word was final. The worst thing was knowing my mum was watching it all. I could barely look at her sitting in the courtroom as I turned to be led out.

All I could think was how her dreams for me would be shattered. Had all her suffering over almost two decades been in vain?

I was devastated by the decision, but not completely surprised. I guess I'd always known in the back of my head that prison was a reality. Dismissed from court, I sat restlessly in my holding cell, waiting to talk to my solicitor about what would happen now, beyond the obvious that I was going to jail. My biggest concern was where I would be placed. That mattered to me. Peckham was rough. The streets were hard to navigate and the lifestyle really took its toll, but jail could be rougher. I'd learned from my friends who'd been inside about how wild it could get. You always had to be ready to fight. People could attack you on your wing with boiling water and sugar, or a snooker ball wrapped in a sock, if you were off guard. I tortured myself with thoughts about what might happen, how I'd mentally survive it all, until eventually Mohammed reappeared.

'You're being sent to Feltham,' he told me. It was hard to imagine that this could possibly be good news, but it was the best news I could have received that day. Feltham Young Offenders Institution wasn't far out of London. I had some friends there. Sodiq, David and Jordan, my co-defendants, were there too. Qudus, another one of my co-defendants, was in another prison in Bristol. I couldn't imagine myself somewhere that far away. More than anything, I didn't want to be alone. It tells you how low I'd fallen that relief swept through me.

I would be transported on a bus with windows I couldn't open – a sign of what was to come when I got to my cell. And when I made the journey I was still in handcuffs, shoved into a locked cubicle with just one large and cushion-less seat that could fit three of me. Like the child I still was, I found myself sliding up and down the oversized seat every time we turned a corner. I could see the out-side world passing by. The cyclists and the drivers all went about their business. And I followed the pedestrians walking, minding their own business, as the prison van made its way through London. I could see them all from my closed window, but no one could see me through the one-way glass. Then I realized: I had become one of the invisibles, no longer a member of society. I'd gone from being seen – someone who was looked up to at college and beginning a life in politics – to becoming just another sorry statistic; a soon-to-be prisoner and an outcast.

Despite knowing that going to prison might happen to me, given the life I was leading, the real-ity of prison had never really dawned on me. I knew the stories and had even visited friends in prison, but you can't understand what it really feels like until your own freedom is taken away. Even as I entered through the heavy gates and the series of doors, each one needing to be unlocked, I still had no idea what really happened behind them.

For the first time ever, I wished I had been caught for something I had actually done. At least it would have been what I deserved. But here I was, eighteen years old, kidnapped by the state and staring at a sentence longer than the life I had already lived.

8

Prison Break

'He was a poor man in a criminal justice system that treats you better if you are rich and guilty than if you are poor and innocent.' – Anthony Ray Hinton, *The Sun Does Shine*

A4690CD.

That was my prison number.

It was given to me not long after I was led from the van, through the front entrance of Feltham prison, and put in a holding room. There, I was asked to confirm my personal details and have my photo taken for my prison ID.

Thinking about that mugshot now, I can see in my eyes how far I had fallen. Dressed in my grey Levi's hoodie and blue jeans I felt worthless, staring glumly ahead as the camera flashed. How did I go from being in the top 1 per cent of students in the country, achieving twelve or more GCSEs, to being a part of the 1 per cent of the population who ended up in prison? But worse was still to come.

With my photo complete, two male prison custody officers led me into another room behind the reception.

'Right, so now we are going to have to strip-search you. Just to make sure you don't have anything on you, like drugs, a mobile phone or weapons,' one officer said, as if this was as normal as the sun rising.

Strip-search? What could I possibly be carrying? My pockets had already been searched and I'd been patted down at the station and at the court. I couldn't have anything on me, could I?

However polite the order, the indignity of the request left me stunned. I'd never been strip-searched before. Immediately, I wanted to shout, 'No way!' but I could see from the deadpan look on the officers' faces that they weren't asking for my consent. My choices were limited: either I got butt-naked willingly in front of two complete strangers to intimately examine me, or they would just use 'reasonable force' to search me instead. I'd heard the stories from friends inside – about how the force could be anything but reasonable. Plus, where were the witnesses? It could be my word against theirs. Besides, common sense told me that these men didn't care much about me at all. I would just have to comply.

'Do you have anything on you that you are not authorized to have?' one officer asked.

'No, I don't have anything on me,' I replied, dreading what might come next.

'Can you please empty your pockets and remove any jewellery, including any wristwatch you may have.'

I emptied my jeans pockets, and I felt some satisfaction in showing them there was nothing there. The other officer stepped close towards me, pulling at the insides of my pockets roughly to double-check. I stared straight ahead.

'Please open your mouth,' he ordered.

I opened my mouth wide.

'And raise your tongue too.'

Puzzled by his demand but not questioning him, I slowly raised my tongue. Then it clicked. People could smuggle things into the prison in their mouths. They left no stone unturned with this search, every inch of me had to be inspected. I couldn't help but wonder how people smuggle mobile phones, drugs and even alcohol into prisons, if these searches are in place?

'Can you now remove your hoodie and any clothing from your top half of your body and pass it to the officer,' the leading officer said, interrupting my thoughts.

I got topless, like some Instagram gym instructor but without the muscles. The room was cold, and the chill air hit me. The other officer searched my clothes while I held my arms up, turning on instruction while the other looked up and down my body, scanning it with a hand-held metal detector. My insides squirmed as he waved the machine across me. I felt so vulnerable.

When the officer returned my clothes, I threw them on quickly, but I couldn't look either of them in the eyes.

'Can you remove your shoes and socks and pass them over.' It all seemed routine for them, but to me every ask felt as agonizing as the last.

Quickly, I pulled off my trainers and socks and shoved them over. I had to lift up my feet one by one and show I had nothing under my toes.

'Can you now remove your trousers and underwear.'

This was the bit I had been dreading. Timidly, I took off my jeans and my boxers. I was horrified. I had never ever felt so degraded. What did I have to show my genitals and my naked self to these officers for? Slowly, I did as he asked, fighting my urge to cover myself, my gaze fixed on the floor.

'Can you lift up your hoodie to your waist and turn around for me.' The officer leaned in and again looked to see if I was hiding anything, as he continued scanning me. Now, I became terrified they would ask me to bend over and search inside of me, my body tensing as I waited for the order.

Thankfully, it never came. The officer who searched my jeans and underwear returned my clothes. They had found nothing. The last thing stripped in this process was my pride.

That day, it seemed like I was taken to room after room. First, my clothes were returned to me and I threw them on, desperate to be warm again, not naked and vulnerable. Later, I would be given an oversized standard-grey jumper, matching grey trousers and green T-shirt. I had worn many uniforms in my eighteen years – and this was the one I would wear in prison, at least until my mum brought me some of my own clothes. Then, in another separate room, I got put before a healthcare professional.

'Have you struggled with substance misuse?' she asked, barely looking up at me from her notes, as if she had somewhere else she wanted to be.

'Nope,' I replied matter-of-factly.

'What about your mental health – have you self-harmed or done so in the past?'

'Nope.'

The questions kept coming and she ticked box after box. Realizing I was just another number for her, I wanted to move through it fast. I could feel my body getting weary the longer I stayed in that room.

'Have you been experiencing suicidal thoughts, or have you done so in the past?'

I was not feeling suicidal, but at this rate I felt I was getting closer to the edge with every question.

'Nope,' I said instead.

'Okay, looks like you're done,' she said, closing her file abruptly. Apparently she wasn't one to dig further. I was placed in yet another holding room, this time with other young men who had just arrived. I acknowledged them with a nod, nothing more. I kept my eyes down and a scowl on my face so no one would talk to me.

'Mr Kenny Eme . . .'

I looked up as a custody officer's shout punctured the silence.

'Eme . . . Kenny Emefidon.'

Is she talking to me? I thought. She'd botched my name badly, so it was hard to know.

'Me?' I put my hand to my chest.

'Yes. You. It's time for you to make your quick phone call.' She emphasized the 'quick'.

I drew a sharp breath before standing up. I knew I had to call my mum. I had to tell her I was here and all right – for now at least anyway. As I punched every digit 0, 7, 9, 4 . . . I exhaled, hyping myself up, trying to lift my mood so that when she heard my voice she wouldn't suss how low I really felt. The last time I'd spoken to her on the phone I had just been charged in Islington Police Station. This time, I was in prison looking at a life sentence. I knew her worry would be unimaginable, so I didn't want to make it any worse. The phone was ringing now, so I pulled myself together. Mum answered in seconds. Clearly, she'd been waiting anxiously for my call all day.

'Hi, Mum, it's Kenny. I'm at Feltham now,' I said, trying to sound as normal as I could.

'How are you doing my boy?' she asked.

'I'm all right, Mum, I just got here and I'm fine. My solicitor will be applying for bail for me in a few days, so hopefully I won't be here long.' I was holding on to the small hope I had that my stay here would be very temporary. I could apply for bail at my next hearing. Mohammed had warned me that the chances of me being granted bail were slim, but there was still a chance and that was all that mattered to me. And the more I said it, the more I believed it. The stress in my mum's voice told me she needed to believe it too.

'Me, Daddy, Grandma, and the family back home are all praying for you,' she said. 'Please read your psalms. Read Psalm 27 every day. And Daddy said Psalm 35 too.'

To be clear, 'Daddy' wasn't my biological father. I would never have expected anything from him. Instead, he was my mum's partner, David, who was also the pastor in our family church. Although I'd known David all my life, my mum and him only got together just before I went to prison. They had been due to get married, but any plans had been put on hold because of my case. In fact, David couldn't be more opposite to my actual dad. He was present, thoughtful and generous.

'I will read them, Mum,' I replied, though I had no Bible.

'Just be prayerful,' she said, sounding more hopeful than me now. 'God is on the throne. Everything will turn out fine in the end.'

I wish I could have said I felt the same.

With my brief phone call over, I was taken to an induction wing called Lapwing. This was one of the twelve wings on Feltham B, if you include the in-patient wing and the segregation unit – 'the block' as it was known. That was the wing boys got sent to if they were causing problems. There, they would have to sit in isolation, and no one wanted to be spending their nights in the block. All the other wings were named after birds: Swallow, Nightingale and Quail, for example. This seemed baffling to me because we were far from free – more like birds in a cage. Feltham was also split into two sides: Feltham A, which held young people aged 15–18, and Feltham B, which held young adults like me aged 18–21. There were just shy of 770 young people in Feltham when I arrived. Most came from all over London, bringing their own issues and feuds from the streets into the prison. Hundreds of angry children and adolescents, with nothing to lose and everything to prove, all in one place. Enemies packed in next to arch-rivals. It made the perfect cocktail for violence, and I knew I had to watch my back.

Finally, when the officer opened the steel cell door and told me this was my room for the night, I just stared at the four concrete walls. All I could see inside was a rusty toilet, a scaled-up sink basin, a cheap white kettle, and a blue plastic mug and a plate with matching cutlery. As far as furniture went, there was a wooden desk, a flimsy chair, a soft brick for a mattress and bed, wrapped in green sheets, and a TV with a screen smaller than my computer at home. It hit me in that moment like a punch from Mike Tyson that any comforts enjoyed at my home were long gone. The only thing to be grateful for was that the cell smelled of nothing. No disinfectant smell, or worse, the stench of a previous inmate.

But this new room was so small it made my box room at home look like a penthouse suite. Immediately, I felt claustrophobic, and the unfamiliar prison jumper began to make my skin itch. I had no mobile phone. I had no connection to the outside world. I had no freedom.

As I gazed through the windows that I couldn't open, I took in the view. It had exactly the same bareness – more concrete prison blocks and dry, unkept grass. And when I turned on my TV, I found out I only had channels 1–5. Not even Freeview. At home, I had been used to Sky and an abundance of choices I took for granted. It would hurt my eyes to see anything in that squashed up screen too. What did I expect? This was not a hotel. This was prison, a place of punishment. But the question that kept spinning round my head was, why was I here? Was I not innocent until proven guilty? I had not been convicted of any crime. Yet here I was, robbed of all my privileges. Why did I have to be punished like a convict if I was on remand?

That night, insomnia gripped me, and I tossed and turned on my single bed. I couldn't stop thinking about the charges over my head that were heavy enough to keep me in here for ever if I was found guilty. The course of my life would be decided by twelve jurors who didn't know me or the truth.

For my first couple of days in Feltham, I was locked up for 24 hours. Time dragged, like wading through a swamp, going nowhere fast, with nothing to keep me company but the background noise of the television. Back and forth I paced, waiting to be moved. *Is this even legal?* I kept asking. *I haven't even done anything.*

Apparently, I was locked in there because officers could not find a space for me yet on another wing, but who knew how long that would take? If I was going to be stuck in here like this until my court date, I didn't know how I would survive.

On the second day, though, I had a distraction, if only for a few moments. The prison chaplain came to check in on me. Our conversation wasn't long, but it made me feel human again, having someone to talk to. Spending time cramped up in this shoebox of a cell had made me crave human connection.

'Do you want a Bible, Kenny?' he asked in a soft voice.

'Please,' I said, thinking about how I just needed to hear from God right about now.

'I'll bring you one,' he reassured me. He told me his name was Graham and maybe because he was a man of God, I was drawn to him. If I had nothing else to do in this cell at least I could read the psalms my mother told me to.

In the meantime, I broke up the days by eating. On my first night, an officer had offered me a 'non-smokers' pack' which contained biscuits, chocolates, and orange squash. I munched through the biscuits and chocolate out of boredom, to fill the craving for something familiar, but in less than two days they were gone. When I didn't get a replacement pack the next day, or the day after that, I asked the officer who brought my lunch when I could expect more.

'You won't get more snacks,' he told me, smirking, 'you'll have to buy them from the weekly prison canteen sheet.' I stared at him in horror. What should have lasted me until my first canteen order next week, I had gone through in just over a day. As soon as the officer turned and left, I collapsed on to my bed, faced the wall, and cursed in disbelief under my breath.

On Lapwing, just like every other wing, I would be given three uninspiring meals a day. To be fed breakfast, lunch, and dinner was a legal requirement promised to all prisoners. But breakfast was far from a full English. It was offered to us in our cell the night before and consisted of non-branded cereal or muesli. Then there were teabags, sugars, and a small carton of long-life milk. Lunch was only hot on weekends – usually I was offered a choice of sandwich, a packet of crisps. The best days were when I was given a bag of onion rings on my tray, and some fruit. Dinner, thankfully, was always a hot meal, though nothing special. They were basic dishes, all of which I could make myself – if I ever bothered to cook – like beef lasagne, chicken Kiev, shepherd's pie or, what became my personal favourite, Betty's Browned-Down Chicken, as it was called. I had no idea who Betty was, but her brown gravy sauce was flavoursome, and tasted of something at least, unlike the other dishes. Not that I was expecting Michelin-star standards – just something that didn't taste ... well, bland. The more I ate this prison food, the more I missed my mum's delicious jollof rice with stewed chicken, and her pounded yam with ogbono soup.

Seventy-two hours after I arrived in Feltham, I was moved out of Lapwing and relocated to Partridge, where I finally got the chance to shower. I'd felt filthy – and I *was* filthy. It had been at least three days since any soap had touched my skin. Never before had I appreciated having a shower so much. It didn't even matter to me that the showers were grimy, with ripped-up soap packaging covering the blue floors. I was just thankful to be stood under hot, running water. On the wing, there were only about eight cubicles between around fifty young men, and when people didn't have slippers they would use their prison shirts as shower mats. Some cubicles were worse than others, and I tried to avoid those where the water sputtered out meekly and ran lukewarm.

Partridge was also the wing where I got my real induction into prison life, both from staff and fellow inmates, who showed me the ins and outs of how to survive. I was in cell number 35, on the lower ground floor of the landing. On either side of me were more cells and there was another floor directly above me. My new cell was a real matchbox, even smaller than my last cell in Lapwing. If I lay on my bed, and stretched out to the other side of the room, I could easily touch the wall. The window was smaller, the view was equally uninspiring – just grey concrete, more rugged, parched grass, and just a sliver of grey sky.

As I lay on my bed that first day in Partridge, I tried to listen to the sounds of the prison, to see what I could learn about the environment: at certain times, I could hear constant movement such as footsteps and voices, when inmates left and returned from work, but at other times there was nothing but an empty, eerie silence. Running through my head were so many questions. Who were my neighbours? Would I bump into someone from another ends who had issues with me? And, the recurring question that had filled my mind from the day I arrived: how was I going to fill my time in here?

Each day, I would only get an hour out of my cell, for what was called 'association'. After spending 24 hours a day alone on Lapwing, this daily freedom felt God-sent. I packed it full with everything I could: shower, make a phone call, play snooker or table tennis or cards, or get to know other people on the wing – not that I was here to make friends.

On my first association, I met Zack and Kwaku. We clicked straight away. Zack had been moved to this wing not long before me. He looked like what we would call a sweet boy – a ladies' man – and far from a threat. Kwaku, on the other hand, was a lamp post of a man, tall with limousine-length feet, who wore a big, innocent smile on his face. Quickly, I learned that everyone you met only cared to know three things about you: what your name was – your real name, or the name that you went by. What ends you were from. And what crime you were inside for. Zack and his co-defendant were both inside for kidnap. Kwaku was in prison for several cash-in-transit robberies that made him and a few of his mates more than £50,000 before they got caught.

'And you?' Zack asked of me. I hesitated. It was the first time I'd said it out loud.

'Murder,' I said. 'Joint enterprise.'

'Rah, that's a big case still.' His eyes widened, and I sensed he was thinking about how he would hate to be me.

I gave him a few more details about my case, but I was careful not to tell him too much, only what had been on the news. Trust isn't overflowing in prison, but I did mention the names of my co-defendants.

Kwaku and I got on like a house on fire, and we ended up sharing a cell together some weeks later. Both Kwaku and Zack showed me love on that first day out on the wing, and I respected them for it. As it turned out, I had just missed that week's canteen order to buy items like toiletries, sweets, and telephone credit for myself – the calls weren't cheap either – and Kwaku and Zack softened the blow by giving me some snacks and toiletries. 'Say nothing,' Kwaku said when I thanked him.

But just as a warm feeling started to fill me up, I noticed out of the corner of my eye someone marching across the room. When the guy, who I'd not seen before, reached the snooker table, he revealed a faded grey sock dangling from his fingers. He was not there to play pool. Instead, he swiped a couple of the balls from the table and stuffed them inside his sock. I tensed, now closely watching his every move. Hiding his hands behind his back, he then walked over to a group gathered in the corner. Whether he was going to attack everyone or not, I didn't know, but it turned out he wasn't aiming for the group at all. Near where they were loitering, a prisoner suddenly came out from his cell. The guy leaned forward, gave a full swing and *douff*!

He crashed the sock into this other guy's cranium. Inside, I winced. That guy would certainly be swapping his prison bed for a hospital bed that night, I figured.

Again, he swung his sock like it was a cricket bat, and now the guy doubled over. The alarm rang out, a deafening siren that filled the whole wing. A swarm of prison officers rushed in to break it up. I was soon to learn that the alarms went off regularly in this place. There was always some fight happening somewhere.

In my cell, I had too much time on my hands and nothing to do with it but think. So much time to think, that I got tired of thinking. My most inescapable thought was that prison was, at its simplest, a poorly run service. It functioned wrong, like a failing business. I had only been there a few days, but I could tell you for free that our prison system is a mess – a true waste of public money. I wondered what percentage of taxpayers would be comfortable knowing that the government is spending an average of nearly £50,000 a year to keep someone in prison who hardly leaves their cell?[1] Why isn't there adequate support to rehabilitate and address the complex needs they might have, such as mental health challenges and illiteracy? For children in custody the costs are even higher, ranging from £76,000 to £210,000 a year for each child locked inside.[2] For me, this is even more disturbing. Do people know their hard-earned money is spent like this? For this amount we could be sending a child to a top private school like Eton, where the annual fees are (at time of printing) just over £45,000. The total annual economic and social cost of reoffending is £18.1bn.[3] Don't let that number go over your head. It's practically the same amount the UK government spends on housing and community development.[4]

So much money is spent to keep us here, but still a high number of inmates return to society having gained nothing during their sentence, except a bigger network to lead them even deeper into criminality on their release.

I was no criminologist or prison expert but, even as I stared, bored, at the walls of my cell, I was sure that as a society we could do much better. I couldn't understand why we didn't look at more alternatives to custody, like community sentences. In England and Wales we imprison more people than anywhere else in Western Europe, and mainly for petty and non-violent crimes which carry sentences of six months or less.[5] Why are we not investing more in preventing those types of crime happening in the first place? Or focusing on wider issues that lead people to crime – like poverty – *before* investing so much in more prison places?

Still, as I settled into my new living arrangements, I was grateful for one thing. I got on well with other residents here, and had made no enemies – none that I knew of at least. Then, I laid eyes on Stefan. Stefan was a tall Jamaican guy I knew from Peckham. I'd never been fond of him on the outside, and the feeling was mutual. We were in the same friendship circle, but he'd got it into his head that his girlfriend and I were doing a thing. We weren't, but try telling him that.

The first time I noticed him was when I was

outside during exercise. The truth is nobody actually did any exercise in the yard. Instead, many of us took the opportunity to have time out of our cells to socialize, get fresh air, or for others to gamble their canteen items. But there, across the yard, I saw the unmistakable shape of his head craning over the other guys he huddled with.

I was shocked. I knew he'd gone to jail, but what were the odds? Of all the jails that exist, and all the wings, this guy from my area would end up on mine. They say it's a small world but depending on what ends you grew up in, prison can seem even smaller. We nodded at each other, communicating the unwritten rule: we were both here now, and from Peckham, so we had to put our differences aside and have each other's backs. There was no beef between us here. I couldn't let him get his face smashed up in front of me and do nothing, and vice versa. Not because I cared about him, but out of principle. We were Peckham Boys, inside and out.

When we eventually spoke, Stefan told me how I could link up with some other Peckham Boys and even see my co-defendants, Sodiq and David.

'Go to the church,' he said. 'Not the Roman Catholic services though, the Church of England ones. That's where they'll be.' Of all the places, and given why we were there, who would have ever thought church would be our meeting point?

That said, he didn't have to tell me twice before I asked one of the wing staff in the office to put me down on the list for church. I had not seen any of my co-defendants – my friends – in months, since they were all arrested for different charges. I would have liked to have seen them in different circumstances, but I was excited, nonetheless. I had something to look forward to for once – and counted out the days on my fingers until Sunday rolled around.

Not long after I talked with Stefan, I was sat in my cell thinking, when I heard an officer's keys hit the lock.

My door swung open.

'You have a visitor,' the officer told me.

'Who?' I asked, intrigued.

'A psychologist,' he replied.

How exciting, I thought, rolling my eyes. It was a visitor, but not one I was thrilled to see. I wanted to see my mum and George. What would I need to see a psychologist for? In a situation like this, what could they possibly do for me, honestly?

As I was led out to a holding room on the wing, I could see a small blonde woman, perhaps mid-thirties. Uninterested in anything she had to say, I slumped down on the blue, budget sofa and gazed at the outdated selection of books on the wooden shelf, deliberately not making eye contact with her.

'How are you, Kenny? Nice to meet you. I'm Cathleen, and I am a clinical psychologist here,' she said softly, holding out her hand to shake.

'I'm good, thanks,' I mumbled. I wasn't going to go out of my way to make her feel welcome. Besides, I wasn't doing good at all, considering where I was, but I wasn't about to tell her how I really felt. The last thing I wanted was for them to put me on suicide watch, on my own in a cell and being checked on and monitored on a regular basis by staff. That would isolate me even further.

'I hope you're settling down well here,' Cathleen continued. 'I am just going to ask you some questions to see how you're doing, if that's all right?'

'Yeah,' I replied. 'That's cool.' She seemed like a nice woman, only doing her job. Her questions started rolling in and my carefully curated answers started flowing. I was diplomatic with her, telling her as much as she needed to hear. I was nervous about my upcoming bail hearing, missing home, but I was exercising and keeping active.

Then Cathleen said: 'On a scale of one to ten, with one being not at all and ten being very happy, how happy would you say you are?'

I faltered. How do you answer a question like that? Well, mate, I thought, how would you feel if you were in my shoes, had just turned eighteen and now were on remand for a murder you didn't commit? If you were looking at a minimum of thirty years of your life behind bars? If you were locked away from the people you love, and had your name splashed all over the news as a murderer? If you were sitting bored to death in a cramped cell for 23 hours a day with nothing to help you pass the time? How happy would you say you were? Truthfully, what was there to be happy about?

'Seven,' I answered, despite my reservations about her stupid question. 'I'm all right.'

Seven was my lucky number, and it felt like a safe number too. Not too happy, but not depressed. It seemed to satisfy her, and when she was finally done with her assessment she seemed confident I wasn't on the brink of a breakdown and happy to close her file and not escalate my case.

'Is there anything I can do for you at all?'

Finally, the moment I had been waiting for. I'd had more than enough time thinking it over in my cell to know what I wanted – if anyone cared enough to ask. If the prison system itself wasn't going to help me better my prospects, I was going to seek them out myself.

'Could you please help me to arrange to have my A level exams done in prison?'

Cathleen's eyes widened a little.

'I've come this far, and I would hate it if I could not sit my final exams,' I continued. I was only months away from finishing college, and I wanted my hard work to be worth something. 'I do not want to get out of here and redo a whole year of college again.'

Cathleen was clearly taken back, but she held on to her poker face and nodded.

'I'll speak to education and they will get back to you,' she said. I didn't realize then, but I was likely the first person who had ever asked her this. In that moment I was just happy to have met someone in this place who seemed open to my request. All I could do was hope that she was a person of her word – like Graham, the chaplain, who came back to see me and dropped off the Bible he had promised. Back in my cell, I turned to Psalm 27, like my mum had asked: *Wait on the Lord: be of good courage, and he shall strengthen thine heart: wait, I say, on the Lord.* But how long would I have to wait here?

As my first week continued I was not doing anything that required energy, so at night I was still struggling to sleep. Insomnia was winning the war against me. I was still adapting to life inside, and I had a lot to learn.

One night officers switched off my electric around midnight as I was watching TV. *What the hell?* I said to myself, screwing up my face at my reflection in the blank television set. I could hear other inmates banging their doors and hurling all types of insults at the officer on night duty (and their mothers, too!) so I knew it wasn't just me. The next morning, when they let me out for association, I went straight to the staff office ready to cause a scene.

'You failed your room check,' they told me before I could get my words out. That's why they had turned my electricity off. My confusion stunned me into silence. What kind of crap is this? Am I in the army or something? The officer informed me nonchalantly that I was expected to keep my cell tidy and clean in time for morning checks. Anything from a little toothpaste stain in the sink to my curtains still being closed could make me fail. I was not allowed to be under my covers when an officer came to inspect my room, either. Even if I didn't have to be at work or education that day, I was expected to be up or lying on top of my duvet. Only enhanced level prisoners, those who have demonstrated good behaviour and were likely to be in positions of trust in the prison so they could carry out special tasks, would never have their electric turned off at night like me.

No one had told me about this before, but that made no difference to the officers. I hoped I would not find myself in this position again – but my real hope, the one that I carried with me every waking moment – was that I would get bail soon and be free from this endless nightmare.

As my first weekend in Partridge approached I now had two things to look forward to. I had never been so excited for church, and to see my friends on Sunday, but more than that I couldn't wait to see my mum. She visited me on the Saturday with David, my soon-to-be stepdad, and George. Sitting together with them in the visiting hall, with my grey prisoner outfit on, was very different to our times sitting together in the living room eating rice and stew with meat. I had never craved my mum's company like this before. I was back to being her baby, and I needed her now more than ever. Not only did I need her support, but the regular postal orders she sent too – prison life wasn't cheap and the cost of making phone calls to her and other people was extortionate. The phone provider was making good profits for sure.

There were a lot of other inmates who also had visits in the same hall. I saw people's parents, grandparents, uncles and aunties, girlfriends, and even children too. Before sitting down, I scanned the room to make sure I did not see anyone I recognized from the outside that I had beef with. There were only a handful of staff around, and I'd heard that it could get popping in the visitor hall. The last thing I needed was someone fulfilling an old vendetta against me and attacking me off-guard while I sat opposite my family on the screwed-down grey chairs.

As I scanned the room to double-check who was there, I heard David kiss his teeth. When I looked over he was slowly shaking his head.

'Look at how many young Black men are here,' he said.

And he was right. Around two thirds of men in that hall were Black, but not because Black men were more likely to be criminals. Young Black men are just more likely to be arrested, charged and sent to prison than young White men. We are over-represented in the prison system, as are other ethnic minority groups. In fact, this systemic racism means that Black men like me are 26 per cent more likely than White men to be remanded in custody, as opposed to being granted bail, and 53 per cent more likely to be sent to prison for an indictable offence at the Crown Court, even when factoring in a higher rate of not-guilty pleas. Walking through a prison like Feltham, you could practically see these statistics hovering over our heads.

When I sat down, it was my little brother George who I felt for the most. He was just a kid, growing into teenage limbs and sitting with the grown-ups now, but still a kid nonetheless. I had moved us out of Peckham to get away from this, so that he wouldn't have to spend his teenage years like I had spent mine, permanently watching over my shoulder. I saw him now, just taking in everything around him, from the other inmates to the officers to the way he looked me up and down. I sensed he wanted to ask me lots of questions but elders being there dampened that urge. In a way, I should have been glad. It was an experience I never wanted him to learn about.

Minutes passed by quicker in the visitor hall than in any other place in prison I'd experienced so far. When an officer shouted, 'Please wrap up your visit', I was surprised. I looked up at the clock to see that our hour was up, but I didn't want it to end.

'What else has been happening at home?' I asked Mum, trying desperately to extend our time together, but I could hear shuffling all around me and knew that sooner or later an officer would be over, telling me to finish up, as if I never heard him the first time. The hardest part was saying goodbye. 'I'll be strong. I promise,' I said to Mum as I hugged her tightly. I didn't want to let go. She held me close, repeating into my ear that she would keep praying for me, and that gave me some comfort. I hugged George and David tightly too, and it struck me then how different our lives would be from that moment onwards. They would be leaving here, stepping out into freedom, while I would be returning to captivity. Worst of all, my little brother would be alone out there. I couldn't even imagine how it felt for him to see me – his reluctant role model – like this. From inside, I couldn't protect him in the jungle.

Before they left, my family said a final prayer for me. David was a businessman but also being a pastor, he had those strong, Yoruba, top-of-mountain prayer points – very deep and meaningful. I certainly needed these prayers as I struggled to pray for myself. But tomorrow was Sunday. 'I'm going to church,' I told them with conviction. It was Sunday, the Lord's day, but I wasn't only going to speak with God. I had other reasons. It was also the day I would see the rest of my brothers. The next morning, despite still struggling to sleep the night before, I woke up feeling revitalized.

As I sat in the church on the wooden chairs with green cushions, I took in this new environment. The prison church was not grimy or filthy like the rest of the prison. The bricks and the decor were all pristine, I noticed, as if it was the one place the cleaners had shown some love.

It was around 9 a.m., and I sat alongside Zack, Kwaku and Stefan waiting for the mandem to enter. Different wings arrived at different times. In Feltham, a place deemed unsafe for boys and staff too, there was no such thing as free-flow. Prisoners couldn't ever make their own way to activities like church, education, or work. If you wanted to go anywhere you had to be accompanied by a member of staff. As every new group arrived, I turned my head in anticipation to see who I recognized file inside.

As soon as I saw the familiar faces – my co-defendants Sodiq, David, and my friend John – I couldn't help but smile, almost as big as Kwaku's usual grin. Although we were not able to catch up, and talk like we usually would, as they were on the other side of the church, I was glad to see them again and exchange the few sentences that we could. 'Yo, bruv, you good?' was about as much as we were allowed. Who ever thought we would all be here together, in prison and in church too? But we all needed God right now, more than ever.

I would go on to attend church every Sunday, apart from the odd week when I couldn't go because security had put me on the 'keep apart' list. This meant that someone somewhere had decided it was either unsafe or just not permitted for me to be in the same place as another prisoner, but I never understood the logic. The decision seemed to change on a whim. At times it would be flagged that another of my co-defendants would be attending a service and so I would be put on the second service, or I'd be told I couldn't attend at all. I'd be fuming in my cell at the injustice – not just because I felt my religious rights weren't being respected, but because I lived for those moments outside my cell, and to see and talk, even if briefly, to my brothers from ends. After all, I was on this wing with no one else I knew but Stefan – and that didn't really count. A lot of the other Peckham Boys were on Swallow wing but I couldn't be transferred there to join Sodiq and the others.

Although in church my main priority had not been to learn about the Bible or Jesus, something strange did happen. Initially, I sat in church feeling encouraged in my spirit, but bored. Growing up in a religious Nigerian household I could not have escaped going to church weekly, so I'd heard all the biblical stories before. I'd always gone with my mum – and even when Mum couldn't go herself – but it was really to keep the peace, especially after she started a relationship with David, which basic-ally made her a pastor's wife-in-waiting. But in Peckham, churches are vibrant, noisy places. Women are dressed so colourfully in their African dresses and *geles* – African headwraps – perched on their heads. From the pulpit, charismatic pastors sell hope and prosperity and the congregation sing loudly to gospel songs and dance to the beat of a drummer like it's a party. Compared to that, much of what went on here seemed very sedate. Many of the special guests who were invited to speak were so uninspiring, just droning on and on. Secretly, I hoped they weren't being paid for their service, because the church should definitely demand a refund.

However, the main preacher, Colin, who was a Black Jamaican man, was different. It didn't take me long to warm to him. He would often say things in that service that touched my spirit and hit home. He would talk about grace and what this meant – the unmerited and undeserved favour of God. He told us that no matter how great our sins, or what we had done to land ourselves in prison, God's grace and forgiveness was greater. What Colin preached just resonated and sparked my interest in this Jesus that characterized love itself. Before long, I had joined a small Bible study group that he led. We would meet every Tuesday and take baby steps in learning more about God. We explored everything from questions like does God exist, to what happens after we die, to why we pray and how to pray.

All this time I had been relying on the borrowed spiritual faith of my mother. But now, I had a safe space to ask childlike questions and not be judged. For once in my life, I was building up my own spiritual foundation, to the point where I was taking it all more seriously every week. Although I had come to accept Jesus as my Lord and Saviour, my problems did not suddenly go away. Far from it. My current situation never changed, not in the slightest. But what did change was that my unstable emotions and anxious spirit began to be replaced by an inexplicable peace.

Colin told me that all the answers to life's problems could be found in the Bible – but I begged to differ. I was learning about forgiving others who had wronged me, which I felt I could possibly do, somehow. But what I was really struggling with was self-forgiveness. What do you do when the person you can't forgive is yourself? I had sold weed for a living. I had violently attacked others who did me no personal wrong, but just happened to be from a different postcode to me. I had slept with numerous women just for the thrill. I was only with them for the here and now, and I was a Casanova with no plans to settle down. I was ashamed of myself. What kind of man was I? And how could I move on while I was wasting my time here in prison? At the end of one session, I asked Colin for a quick word.

'So, what it is, yeah, I am struggling to see how any of my time here is at all productive. My life is not moving forward here. How am I ever meant to catch up with everyone else, when I get back out there? My friends will be starting university in October. But I will be starting my trial. Even if I get out, which I hope to God I do, how will God give me this time back?'

Colin listened intently, but he didn't seem

troubled by the question. He replied without a trace of uncertainty in his voice, as if God had told him directly, 'Joel 2:25. God will recover the time back for you. He will make it all worth it.'

I rolled my eyes and thought: *How though? What makes you so confident?*

Colin turned to Joel 2:25, and showed me the passage:

And I will compensate you for the years that the swarming locust has eaten,
The creeping locust, the stripping locust, and the gnawing locust—
My great army which I sent among you.

'God will recover the time you lost in here and give you back even more for your troubles. Meditate on this scripture and find comfort in it,' Colin said.

I didn't even try to argue or ask him how God could possibly do that. I had learned to understand by now not to be concerned with the 'how' of what God was going to do. I just had to blindly and completely trust in this all powerful being I couldn't see, which was foreign to me.

As I thought more about my spirituality, I thought more too about my life's purpose, and it inspired me to remain focused on my studies. I still wanted to sit my A level exams, but so far things were proving difficult. At the time the prison had only ever accommodated GCSEs, for the younger boys in Feltham A. They had never come across someone like me. Nobody I spoke to, not the officers nor Cathleen the psychologist seemed able to help me. As time went by, and May rolled into June and the exams edged closer, I was becoming convinced that my dream was over.

Though, I did have a flicker of hope.

Into my first month at Feltham, I met Anna, the librarian in the education block. Everyone was given the opportunity to go to the library if they wanted to and I grabbed it. Any reason to be out of my cell, but also my studies were on my mind. I pleaded with her that I wanted to do my A levels and needed help. Being part of the education department, I thought if anyone was going to help me, it could be her.

'Cathleen has already told me about you,' she said. 'A levels are an unusual request in here.' And there I was thinking Cathleen had forgotten all about me, but I was pleasantly surprised that she had followed through on her words.

'Leave it with me. There's another woman I need to speak to and see if we can make this happen,' Anna said. I raised my eyebrows hopefully but inside I felt less confident. I didn't want to feel as though I'd been fobbed off by another person. Why couldn't anyone see how important this was?

But Anna kept her word and she worked surprisingly quickly, too. She introduced me to Joan Hodgson, a bubbly middle-aged GCSE teacher who worked in the prison. She had a smile every time we met. To the naked eye, Joan was human like everyone else. But to me, she was my guardian angel.

Over the next couple of weeks Joan became my advocate. She spoke to the head of education at Feltham to take my case forward and make things happen for me. But it was a hard fight, a trial in itself. The system just wasn't set up to provide that level of education – or to think inmates would want to pursue learning at that level. More than 50 per cent of people who end up in prison either can't read or struggle to.[6] Six in ten regularly truanted while in school, and 42 per cent of the prison population were either expelled or permanently excluded from school.[7] So, the odds of anyone looking to do A level exams here were slim to none.

At first, my college were also resistant, and refused to work with the prison. Maybe they were ashamed of me, or they just did not want to help a suspected murderer. But the head of education backed me, as did Joan, whose determination that I should sit my A levels was almost as strong as my own. My case was fought hard, and eventually my college reversed their decision.

The next issue was how I would prepare for them. My study notes and schoolbooks were all still at my home in Islington. Yet Joan was adamant I would succeed. Despite it being above and beyond her job description, she cheerfully went out of her way to contact my mum and arrange to meet her outside of the prison to get my books, which my mum had retrieved herself from my bedroom. Where the system wasn't working, these women put in the work themselves to make things happen for me.

There was no classroom for me to study in, no other guys preparing for their A levels that I could share the process with. But the long hours I spent in my cell now had a purpose. Evenings passed quickly as I went over and over the books and all the notes my mum could find, trying to remember everything I'd learned in college over the last two years.

With Joan's determination, care and belief in me, I was about to become the first person in Feltham to sit my A level exams. And as I continued to study, hunched over my desk in my cramped cell, my legal team were working just as hard to make sure I wasn't put away for murder.

9

How Do You Plead?

'When I'm at the bottom looking up, the main question
may not be "how do I get out of this hole?" In reality,
the main question might be "how do I get rid of the
shovel that I used to dig it?"' –
Craig D. Lounsbrough, *A View*
from the Front Porch

My mum wrote me a letter while I was in prison.

The woman is really sharp, but not on paper. She can just about put a text together, so getting a letter from her was a big deal. This was her first and only letter to me. It was short, and far from poetry, but the few lines she wrote impacted me like it was a few pages.

I spoke to Mum regularly on the phone and so I didn't quite understand why she felt compelled to write to me, but she did, and it touched me deeply.

She started by reminding me, as she regularly did, to read my psalms – Psalms 9, 27, and 35, to be specific. These reaffirmed God's place as a saviour in times of trouble. But these were psalms that I'd read before. It was when she went on to share her own personal message of love and sorrow, and how she had total faith in me being released, that my tears fell on to the page. As I read on, I couldn't hold them back.

I never cried when I was arrested for murder. I never cried when I was charged with murder. I also never cried when I first came to prison and knew that I could be spending the next three decades of my life inside. I was told big boys didn't cry, so I never did – no matter what I was feeling.

Yet, this short, handwritten letter floored me. The tears kept flowing.

Mum's letter never said it explicitly, but I could read between the lines. I sensed that if she could swap places with me to take my pain away, she would have. Her own strength gave me hope, and my mother's faith reminded me of my own.

It also reminded me that I was not the only one living this nightmare. For that reason, I wanted to make her proud of me, to achieve something despite being inside, so I doubled down on preparing for my A levels. The exams had come around fast. While my classmates would be settling into an exam hall, with tables lined up next to each other, I was on my own in an airy room in a prison. The wing had a few private rooms – one where I met the psychologist, and another one that was linked to the wing officers' offices. It was in this second room where I took my exams. A few of the education staff acted as my invigilators, and I think it was as much of an experience for them as it was for me. When I turned in my final paper to finish, the head of the education department even shook my hand.

Now, I turned to my next immediate hurdle – my bail hearing. It took one month and seventeen days for it to come around, at the end of June. Naively, when I first entered Feltham, I'd thought I would only be in prison for a matter of days before I got my hearing and could make a case for bail. Now weeks had dragged by, and I was ready to get it over and done with.

I did not appear in court in person. Instead, I was taken to a location in the prison that I hadn't known existed, to join the court via webcam. Apparently, this was common for people on remand in prison. When I was asked what my plea was for each of the seven charges against me, I took a deep breath, held my nerve and replied:

'One count of murder,' said the judge.

'Not guilty.'

'Two counts of attempted murder.'

'Not guilty.'

'Two counts of grievous bodily harm.'

'Not guilty.'

'Possession of a firearm.'

'Not guilty.'

'Possession of an offensive weapon . . .'

Once the final *not guilty* left my mouth, I knew I had to bury any dream of getting bail and going home soon. Hearing the charges read out like that again, it really hit home how seriously they were stacking the odds against me. I would be here until a trial was scheduled, and then a jury would decide my guilt or innocence. The list alone sounded brutal, I could hear it myself – what if a jury decided I was lying with my not guilty plea? It would be game over. The only way I would be going home now would be if they believed me.

The trial date was set for the week of 17 October 2011. It was only June. Knowing this would be my home for another few months meant that I began to settle into prison life more seriously. Without my exams to keep me occupied, I did my best to desensitize myself to the horror of this nightmare.

My strategy was simple. Just keep busy. So, I did everything I could to fill my time so that at the end of each day, I could lay down tired.

The library became the place I went often, to borrow books to take back to my cell. And books became a great escape. I developed an interest in the author Dan Brown, whose book *The Lost Symbol* became one of my favourites. He was a real

storyteller and his style captivated my imagination. I'd lie in my cell painting vivid pictures in
my head of the places he described that I had never
seen.

My small TV also became a good friend, even
without my usual selection of channels to choose
from. Nevertheless, I indulged in anything from
EastEnders to *Loose Women* for my lunchtime treat
(don't judge me!). Surprisingly, evening game
shows also became my bag. Not programmes I'd
ever watched before. But no matter how bored I
was, I just couldn't bring myself to watch *Emmer-
dale* or *Hollyoaks*.

And, it's amazing what you come to enjoy when
the days stretch out so long. Although I could play
the albums I had on CD from artists like Rick
Ross, Drake and Wiz Khalifa, I also got to love a
song that was played on the radio constantly called
'Glad You Came' by a band called The Wanted. It
wasn't really my kind of music but it was played
religiously on lots of stations, and before I knew it,
I was a fan of the song. In fact, it became my guilty
pleasure.

I reckon a lot of the boys on the wing developed
guilty pleasures just like me. Aside from artists like
Jay-Z and Kanye West, whose album *Watch the
Throne* was released that summer, Adele's album *21*
was also in high demand. That summer, there were
lots of boys in their cells lost in the sound of

heartbreak, probably dreaming about seeing loved ones and girlfriends again.

I loved music and how upbeat it could make me feel. Most times I blasted my music out with no respect for others. Suddenly, the bass from Kanye's 'All Of The Lights' would vibrate through the walls and I'd tune out, reciting every word and nodding to every beat, just as if I was at a club or in my room at home.

But other things reminded me of home too much. In prison, I could only play old-school PS2 games, but every time I did I thought about being back in Peckham and competing against George on Xbox, or being at my friends' places, chilling, catching up on hood gossip, while our hands grasped the controls and we tried to kill as many zombies as we could until our eyes got tired.

Inside, these small moments felt like freedom, whereas the brain-dead educational courses in English and the arts felt so dry to me – nothing like the politics I was passionate about, or anything I had learned on my college courses. Honestly, the most challenging task I was given in English was to write a short essay about 'Life Without a TV'. I was in prison so my imagination didn't have to run far. In my art class I just drew – or more accurately traced – photos of *Lion King* characters. A simple task, but I tried to take pleasure in my young Da Vinci-like skills.

As for exercise, I lived for the times when I could sweat and burn off some of the anger frequently boiling inside of me. Of course, I played football at every opportunity, whether inside the gym hall or outside in the big field. But I also played rugby. Now, I'm a slim guy. Not your typical built-for-rugby type on the surface, but I had played rugby when I was younger and for my school team, too. Some players were double my size, and others were steroid-looking, I-bench-150kg-for-a-warm-up-exercise gym fanatics, but I played to my strengths. Unlike a lot of first-timers who played rugby in the prison, I was good at the tackles, so the size of the others did not intimidate me. Rugby is as much about technique as it is about strength, and there is one place where all men are equal – the ankles. It's where a young David like me could focus, when trying to take Goliath down.

As far as making friends was concerned, I would sometimes share a double cell with another Feltham resident, but never for too long. I would only share a cell with someone who I really got along with and who had my back in there. This helped time pass too. Me and my cellmates would talk about anything and everything. We would share stories and memories about moments in the hood, girls, and what we would do when we got out. Thankfully, double cells were not always as compact as single cells. You had a bit more space and a bunk bed. Unlike what you see in the movies, there was no big fight over who slept on the top or the bottom bunk – not in my case anyway. However, in Feltham, various wings did have what we called the penthouse. These were super-spacious cells on the top landing of the wings and situated in the corner. Although these cells were for two people, they could easily fit between four and six, and for that reason they were highly sought after. Unfortunately, I never stayed a single night in one of the penthouse suites, but Sodiq and John, who were on Swallow wing, did – lucky lads. And while the company of a cellmate would help to keep my mind off things, I would often crave my own space. There's only so much of smelling someone else's logs in the toilet a man can take.

I also longed to work in prison, just to keep me occupied and feeling useful, but I had to wait. From the earliest opportunity I had put my name down to work, but there were no jobs available. It took me a couple of months, but I eventually got a job working in the main kitchen. This new job was well paid, too, by prison standards: £10 a week, which could buy you all sorts of goodies on the prison canteen sheet. The only better-paying job was in the officers' mess, serving prison staff who were there to eat and socialize. One perk for those who worked there was being able to eat toast, a treat no other prisoner had, as we never had access to a toaster.

But working in the kitchens was far from the glamorous job I had imagined it to be. I'd never been a good cook, but that didn't seem to matter as there seemed very little chance for me to cook anything. Occasionally I got the chance to stir the crappy soup they were making. Much of my job involved collecting things from storage or the walk-in freezer rooms, and moving things around the kitchen. I was also a human dishwasher and was tasked with washing countless trays and kitchen utensils. I would do whatever was required by the kitchen staff, and they were not short of tasks to give me.

What was better for me, though, was that my new job also came with a change of wing. To be closer to the kitchen, I was moved to Teal, which was closer to the gym too. Deep down, I really wanted to move to where most of my friends from Peckham were, but the prison security blocked any hopes of that. However, I wasn't exactly crying about this move. Teal was known as the best wing in the prison. There were fewer people, and bigger portions of food. It was cleaner, and we would regularly be offered extra gym sessions, which meant more football for me. Everyone was on the same floor and the wing sat right above healthcare – not that this meant you could see a nurse any quicker.

Thankfully, there was also hardly ever any trouble on Teal. And I did my best to keep the peace flowing through there, to keep it comfortable. Sometimes, I would see boys who looked unable to defend themselves allow others to push in front of them in the phone queue. I found that difficult to watch because it felt unfair to me. So, I'd tap the shoulder of the guy who was on a call and make sure he gave that boy his turn first when he'd finished. Other times, I stepped in if I saw someone being bullied or mocked who was in no position to hold their own. It was the school prefect in me jumping out – I had never liked bullies on the outside and I never liked them in prison either.

We were all serving time in our own way, even the prison officers. But on Teal even they were friendlier, although like everyone in a prison, they had their days. I got on well with most, if not all, of them. One time I even gave Mr Harris some snacks from my own canteen order, as he was starving and had to skip his breakfast before coming to work after rushing to drop his daughter off at school. You don't usually hear stories like this, but positive community spirit can and does exist inside prisons, even between residents and officers.

Despite the circumstances I was living in, I tried my best to find a reason to smile and even more reason to laugh and banter with others. I was known to be a serial piss-taker, and I was ready to clap back to any joke thrown at me. Being on Teal I felt that, if things stayed like this, I'd be all right. I just had to make it through until my trial.

But less than two months in, something happened which left me so low-spirited. One morning I waited for my door to be opened for work, but no officers came. *Maybe they forgot about me today*, I thought. I pressed the bell in my cell to get the wing staff's attention.

One of the part-time prison officers approached my cell. He was a pale White man in his sixties, but had earned the name Mr Miyagi on account of him showing us some bad karate moves once.

'Mr Miyagi, I've got work. Aren't you opening my door?' I said, confused.

'Sorry, Kenny,' he said apologetically through the hatch. 'You're not going to be working in the kitchen any longer.'

'Why?' I shouted. I could feel the anger rising up inside of me. This was the daily routine I looked forward to, that got me out of my cell in the morning. Besides, I had been doing my job well and had carried out every task that was asked of me. Why was I being punished?

'Powers that be, Kenny. It's because of security.' He raised his eyebrows, signalling to me that even he thought it was unfair. Apparently, I'd suddenly been deemed 'too high risk' to be working

there. Given my risk profile, I should not be surrounded by knives and other sharp objects. I was
sacked with immediate effect.

This felt devastating, and just plain cruel. Yet
again, security was just making my life harder. Why?
All I wanted was to keep myself busy until my trial.
I'd been working in the kitchens for nearly two
months by this time – if I'd wanted to do anything
silly or dangerous, I would have done it by now. I
would have hoped they could trust me after a clean
run of no issues in prison. But they never did.

I went from being employed to unemployed,
just like that. I was back to spending 23 hours a day
in my cell, watching Jeremy Kyle every morning as
he talked down to whichever guest they'd pulled
out for the show. I was furious. On the days when
I would hear everyone else's cell door bang open
and footsteps pacing down the corridor to work,
or the education block, or a workshop, I would be
filled with rage, my leg tapping restlessly and my
fists clenched.

The injustice of it stung harder the longer it continued. I had become so used to being out of my cell
for a big part of the day that it felt like torture. It
was like being grounded by your parents and having
to stay inside while you heard the shrieks and laughs
of other kids playing outside freely.

I even complained to the prison's independent
monitoring board, whose role is to monitor the

day-to-day life and ensure that prisoners are treated fairly and humanely. Well, I certainly felt that what had happened was unfair and inhumane. But they couldn't do anything to reverse security's decision. In the end, I stopped sulking and decided to take another approach. It took me a while, but after some sweet-talking and playing the peeved-and-not-afraid-to-hide-it inmate, I was eventually given another job as a wing worker.

In this job, I would help with brushing and mopping floors, washing clothes, serving food, handing out canteen sheets and other tasks. Unlike in the kitchens, I couldn't leave the wing, but if I finished my work early I could make calls to the outside world on the prison phone – if I was granted permission, of course. It was always made clear that this was not a privilege any of us were allowed to abuse. And it wasn't until I started doing this job that I learned how to use a washing machine properly. At home, my mum had always washed my clothes, and I'd taken no interest in the process at all. One of my jobs was to wheel the laundry, piled up in a trolley bin, to the industrial machines. This happened a few times a week and as I gathered up the bedclothes to load the machines, it struck me how unhygienic and dirty some men were. Some bedsheets were sopping wet and the stench of stale piss hit my nostrils. I was stunned to realize that there were young men in here, aged between eighteen and twenty-one, still pissing their bedsheets.

I also learned how to mop properly using the number-8 technique. This was not the half-hearted mopping I did at home, when asked by my mum. Instead, I was shown how to start at the top of the floor and glide the mophead in figures of eight downwards so not an inch went unwashed. In the end, the rhythm became quite calming. Another thing I was exposed to was how little people lived on. When I handed the canteen sheets out to residents, I could see how much money people had to spend – mainly £5, £12, and £15. Most of this would be money they earned from attending education or working in the prison. I thought: aren't your friends and family on the outside looking after you? Did people on the outside think life in here was easy, and things were free? How did they think their loved ones survived? I was blowing as much as £20–30 a week just on credit to make calls and stay connected with the outside world. I could only imagine how they were feeling. It couldn't have been any good for their morale.

As for me, I had to keep a positive attitude. I had to be hopeful. I had to be prayerful that my time here was only temporary.

I had to behave like someone who was here briefly.

I knew if I got convicted, I would be settling

here for a very long time. But I was not here to settle.

Because I had that mindset, it was one of the reasons why I never bought a small carpet for my cell, or other home comforts. Other inmates there for the long haul had items to make the bareness of their cells seem just that little bit warmer – photographs of girlfriends or wives or families stuck to the wall, or posters. And I understood why, too. If I was going to be here for a while, I would have made myself feel a bit more at home in my personal space. However, I was not planning to be there any longer than I needed to, so a small carpet was never on my shopping list.

I was operating on faith.

Not many days in prison are memorable. They blur from one into the next, and sometimes hot lunches are the only way you realize it's a weekend. But Saturday 6 August 2011 certainly stuck, and the few days following it. I watched the TV in my cell in astonishment as London was burning down. Pictures flashed up of young men throwing petrol bombs, smashing shop windows. Women with children in buggies parked outside raided shops, taking anything from breakfast cereals to nappies. Police in riot gear edged their way down streets with one hand holding their plastic shield against their chests, the other hovering on their truncheons. Riots like I'd never witnessed before.

The wave of violence had been sparked by the killing of Mark Duggan, the 29-year-old who had been shot by police in Tottenham two days earlier. All the reports questioned whether Duggan had had a gun in his hand at the time of the shooting, as it was initially claimed by police. They said they had received information that he was a gang member in possession of a firearm, and was planning an attack, and that's why they chased down the minicab he was travelling in. Some years later an inquest jury would find that Duggan had thrown a weapon from the cab window moments before he was stopped, and was unarmed when he was shot twice by an officer.

In the hours after his death, Duggan's family and friends were rightly seeking answers from the police. They, along with friends and residents from Tottenham, had led a three-hundred-strong peaceful protest from nearby Broadwater Farm to Tottenham Police Station, demanding that a senior police officer speak to them. But they waited for hours only to be told they had to come back another day. Not long after that, violence broke out. Alongside the rest of the UK, I sat open-mouthed for five nights straight at the biggest uprising England had seen for a generation.

Of course, I had heard about the Brixton riots of 1981 and 1985, but I had never witnessed anything close to it in London. From Tottenham, the violence spread to other parts of London, including Brixton, Hackney, Lewisham, Croydon, and where I was from – Peckham.

Desperate to know more, I called my friend Mide as soon as I could get to the prison phone. It was one of those times I wished we'd been allowed mobiles, just so I could get a running commentary, but that was never an option. When I did finally get hold of him I could hear the crowds of angry looters shouting around him.

'It's crazy out here fam. Everyone is just on a mad ting,' he told me. It sounded like he was in the middle of the Wild West. On Rye Lane people were stealing, destroying and burning stuff. JD Sports, Argos, jewellery shops and other local shops had been ransacked – no shops were safe. The police were also under pressure to contain the situation.

Before you knew it the uprising spread like a pandemic to towns and cities across England. People started rioting in Birmingham, Salford, Manchester, Liverpool and Nottingham, and the violence didn't really die down until Thursday the following week. By this time, five people had tragically lost their lives, while hundreds of people and officers were injured and over £200m worth of damage had been done to shops and businesses in London alone. It even spread to Feltham prison.

As we all watched the action on our TV screens over days, some inmates' own frustrations boiled over. All I knew of it was when we were suddenly ordered back to our cells. This was an unusual request and I thought, *what has happened now?* It emerged that a small group of men had gone on a rampage and smashed up the gym. Then we heard that they'd climbed on to the roof and were refusing to get off. Eventually, it took a riot squad to force them down. The only upside was that because no one had been able to enter the kitchens, no cooking had been done and we all got to eat takeaway fish and chips that evening, which made a welcome change from the usual bland selection.

Not long after the riots ended, we started seeing truckloads of people turning up at Feltham. It seemed like court judges were sending almost everyone who had been involved to prison. And, they were handing out longer sentences than usual to people. To me, some of it seemed very heavy-handed. For example, one 23-year-old student with no previous convictions was sent to prison for six months after pleading guilty to stealing bottles worth £3.50 from Lidl in Brixton. It seemed like the judges and politicians were determined to make an example out of everyone caught in this moment of lawlessness. I'd already observed how broken the system was, and this just confirmed my beliefs. Day after day, new inmates arrived. It all felt a bit pointless. No one seemed interested in facing some of the real issues that led to the riots in the first place, like people's frustrations at issues such as policing and race relations. Also that people in poor, neglected areas like Peckham were resorting to having to steal everyday items from shops. Didn't anybody question why? Many of those arrested were remanded in prison awaiting trial, or given longer sentences than they would normally have been if they pleaded guilty. By the end of August, while I was still waiting to find out my A level results, the police had arrested almost 3,000 people for riot-related crimes.

On the morning of A level results day I rang my friend Dan. I'd been at secondary school with him, and also at college. He was a funny guy who we called Little Dan on account of his shortness. I trusted him. He'd kept in touch while I was inside, and I needed someone I felt comfortable with to share this moment.

'Yo, bro, you good yeah?' I asked him.

'Yeah, bro, I'm good. How you holding up?'

'I'm good, bro,' I said, getting straight to the point as I couldn't bear waiting any longer to find out. 'I beg you go online, check my account and see my results.' Dan had not even checked his own results yet, but he could tell I was in a hurry to know mine. I knew I wasn't going to be able to start university that summer, but I just needed to know whether I'd passed or not.

'What are your details so I can log in?' Dan asked.

As I gave Dan my password, my heart raced. I had always been a high achiever and I didn't want to fail now, despite my circumstances.

'Yeah, I am in now bro . . . errr . . . I am just looking, hold on.' Either Dan was buying time or trying to give me high blood pressure.

'You got a D for philosophy, C for politics, and D in your history,' he said, no shock in his voice.

Immediately, I felt overwhelmed with embarrassment. Those Ds only made me feel like one word – dumb. What good or top university would accept me with these grades? Though I had technically passed my exams, it felt like failure. I couldn't bring myself to believe that these were my final grades. In prison or not, I thought I would have achieved better than this.

However, I had to catch myself and remind myself of a few things. Firstly, I hadn't had the same level of preparation you would usually have right before an exam, and secondly, I hadn't had the resources I needed. Thirdly, I was the first person *ever* to get the chance to even do A levels in this prison, especially with the weight of such a big case on my shoulders. That, in itself, was an achievement. I had to stop being so hard on myself.

But I couldn't help it.

'You there, bro?' Dan asked gently.

'Yeah, I am, thanks for letting me know. I am happy still. I passed,' I replied. To mask my disappointment, I put on an upbeat voice, but the truth was I wasn't that happy. As I walked back to my cell, I kept torturing myself with how different I would have felt had my grades been better. After a few hours sat in silence, I turned my attention elsewhere. Although I had officially got my A level worries out the way, there was still one more battle left for me to fight, and that was the case the state had against me. We were less than two months away from the trial now, and the stakes were high. The inevitable was edging closer and I had to be prepared.

10

On Trial for Murder

'Faith sees the invisible, believes the unbelievable, and receives the impossible.' – Corrie ten Boom, *Jesus is Victor*

Wednesday 19 October 2011

After five months in this place, my day of judgement had come. I woke up at around 4.30 a.m., put on some gospel music, and prayed in my cell. It calmed me and stopped my mind from spinning. I'd had a rough sleep that night – as rough as my first few nights in prison.

I had to brace myself for the day ahead. I knew what was coming was nothing like I had ever experienced before. I had never been on trial before, let alone on trial in a Crown Court, and now I would be in the Old Bailey – the court where some of the most serious criminal cases in the country had been heard for centuries.

I put on the shirt and trousers that my mum brought for me to wear, so I would look presentable. I should have had a haircut inside Feltham, but I'd kept my mini Afro. Stubbornly, I committed to not having a haircut until I left this place. I wanted to see the time it had robbed from me, and for others to see it too.

Early in the morning, before 6 a.m., was the time I needed to be ready for processing out of Feltham. A prison officer opened my door and signalled it was time to go. Other men on the wing who were also going to courts were congregating by the staff room and I saw that they looked as tired and displeased as I was to wake up at this ungodly hour. My trial could last as long as eight weeks and I already felt both mentally and physically exhausted. So, I knew that waking up this early every morning would take its toll.

In the same way as I'd entered the prison all those months ago, I was strip-searched on the way out. My heart sank. It had been such a degrading and dehumanizing process the first time around, and now I would have to endure it again. I took a deep breath, knowing it was no way to start the day, but I was also well aware that saying 'no' was not an option.

Outside, when the door opened on the Serco

bus that was to take me to the Old Bailey, I stepped into line with the others, including David and Sodiq. I'd seen them in the waiting room by the reception entrance beforehand and I went to hug them, like a parent at an airport saying goodbye to a child who was emigrating. I could feel their pain as much as I could feel mine. And I could also feel our hope. Though I knew that I would be seeing them again, we all knew that the fight for our lives was about to begin, and that not everyone might make it. Our hugs in that moment said more than words ever could.

Placed into our separate cubicles in the van we headed towards the big steel gate and the outside world, a world I had not seen outside of my dreams in the past five months. As we drove towards London, I greedily took in as much as I could, from drivers and passengers chatting in cars, to lorries and vans bringing early morning deliveries into the capital, and motorway signs all headed towards central London. Suddenly, I found a new appreciation for everything I could see. From the prison, I never saw anything but dry grass, high walls and occasional blue skies.

When we arrived at the Old Bailey, we entered through a secure entrance where remanded inmates came in. I had never seen so many people in bright yellow and blue E-man jumpsuits, being escorted with chains on their hands and feet. These were the highest category risk of prisoners, and you could only imagine what crimes they were there for. Did they blast someone in the head with a shotgun? Did they hack someone to death with a machete? Or were they here on terrorism charges?

My curiosity evaporated as soon as I entered the courtroom. Now, I became less concerned about them and more concerned about what I was there for – a murder and six other charges.

'All rise!' the clerk shouted.

I shot straight up and so did the six others on trial alongside me. Then I watched as the judge entered with his black silky gown and horsehair wig on. He did not smile but neither did he frown. His poker face was fixed.

When I looked around the room, all I could see were wigs, white-haired and curly. Each of us on trial had our own barrister and a QC, which is a senior barrister, to represent us. My barrister was a man called Matt Lefteris. Even though there were a dozen of these people on our side, I had that sinking feeling that we were still the underdogs.

Until the judge sat down, no one moved. Then my six co-defendants and I took our seats.

It is a strange fact of joint enterprise that your life can hang in the balance with people sat beside you that you've barely even met. My co-defendants were a mixture of friends, acquaintances, and strangers.

Sodiq and Qudus were friends of mine, as was David. David was my age, as stubborn as a goat, and could be quite extra – whether it was arguing among friends or chatting up a girl, he took things to the next level, but we all liked him. David was from a Zimbabwean background, which was very different to most of our friendship circles – his surname was a mouthful even for me. He and some of our close friends would come to my house often, partly because they loved my mum's pounded yam with ogbono soup, and her endless supply of supersized Supermalt.

I had only known Jordan for about a year or so, and he was a few years younger than the rest of us, a similar age to my brother. He had his own friends but would like to hang around with us, just as I used to hang around with Dwayne and Femi, though I wasn't in their age group. I liked Jordan. Sometimes I found him annoying, but he was just young. Before he got charged, I never really got to know him but now I had to – this case made us closer than ever.

The final two defendants were young brothers, Gabriel and Emmanuel, who I had never met before in my life. While I was in prison, it had been brought to my attention that the pair had been added to our trial, with the prosecution arguing that the brothers had knowingly assisted Jordan in hiding the gun used in the murder. The police had carried out a search of their house and the surrounding area, in relation to another entirely separate case, and found a drawstring JD Sports bag containing a 9mm loaded handgun stuffed into a sock. An expert examiner said that: 'the gun *could* have fired the missile' that killed the victim in our case. But also that they were '*unable entirely* to discount the possibility that another gun was used to fire it.' This weapon may not be the murder weapon in our case, but the police were going to stick it on us regardless.

These brothers being added to our case was not helping us at all.

Seven people. All Black teenagers. All from Peckham. This was not a good look.

With the judge in his seat, the next job was to select the jury. All I was hoping was that the twelve men and women who would hear our trial were not all White or elderly people. Confronted by young Black men, people in these demographics would surely be more likely to resort to stereotyping us, and that would surely affect their judgement, I felt. I did my best to avoid eye contact with the potential jury members. I did not want to be smiling, as if I smiled it could look bad. On the other hand, if I looked sad or unhappy, that could be mistaken for looking guilty. So, I tried my best to adopt a blank, expressionless face just like the judge's.

Once the judge finished his well-rehearsed script about what was expected of the jurors, and they had been sworn in, the prosecution opened with their case. The lead prosecutor, Duncan Penny, with his black, rectangle glasses, began with the prosecution's story of what happened the night Sylvester was murdered.

A group of youths, he said, gesturing towards us, had entered a block of flats in the Pelican Estate, claiming they were members of a gang from Brixton looking for a rival Peckham gang. Sylvester was part of neither, but had been on an upper floor of this block with two of his friends. The approaching group then split. One group stayed downstairs to guard the doors while another ran upstairs. Not long after, Sylvester was being pursued through the building by this group, armed with a loaded handgun, and was fatally shot in the neck with a single bullet 'somewhere between the fifth and fourth floors'.

The group who had been guarding the doors then 'came ready for the task in hand' and a good number of them had knives. They blocked an exit when they 'stood sentry' on a stairwell. As Sylvester lay dying his friends were 'stabbed repeatedly' as they tried to leave the block, Penny described. He paused. 'Each of them was lucky to escape.'

As I listened to the prosecution's version of what happened that afternoon, I squirmed inside, but tried hard to keep my face neutral. The case was held together by circumstantial evidence and, in parts, fiction to fill in the gaps. However, the way Penny spoke so eloquently and confidently, you would think everything he was saying was gospel. He really believed what he was saying too. You would have thought he had witnessed the whole event himself.

Matt, my barrister, had warned me beforehand that Penny was one of the Crown Prosecution Service's best guys. He'd been up against him once before in a previous trial. 'How did the case turn out?' I'd asked him nervously, just in case I could latch on to any hopeful sign. Thankfully, Matt had won. At the same time, I prayed that Duncan Penny wasn't gunning to get him back for that loss now.

The more Penny spoke, the more guilty we all looked. Yet I also knew that the evidence against me was only based on the mobile phone data, which showed I was in communication with one of my co-defendants around the time of the murder, and also my phone signals placed me in 'the vicinity of the murder'. All of this was wholly circumstantial evidence, nothing material. Basically, the prosecution was saying that if my phone signal was in the 'vicinity' of the crime scene, and I was in communication with other suspects, the jury could draw their own conclusions about where I was and what I was doing. There was no DNA evidence, no CCTV, no witness testimonies, no concrete evidence found against me. The GP surgery where I had waited for George was very close to the building where the murder had taken place, as was Qudus and Sodiq's house. Communication between me and my co-defendants didn't prove anything we didn't already know. I'd never denied knowing them or talking to some of them on the day of the murder, just like we did on any other day. Besides, if I was with them at the crime scene why would I need to call any of them?

The cell-site analysis showed – exactly as I had remembered – that I had been near the area all day. But that did not make me a murderer. Just as I had stated plainly and clearly in my defence statement, I was at home when it happened. I didn't kill anybody. But they were throwing everything they could at me, including the kitchen sink. Still, my alibi was simple and true.

However, the case for Sodiq, David and Qudus was a bit more complex. There were two key witnesses who were together with Sylvester on the day – these were the guys who were stabbed in the stairwell. The main witness alleged, in evidence given before the trial, that he saw Sodiq, David and Qudus at the scene. However, he never picked Sodiq and Qudus out in an ID parade. The second witness claimed that the boys who came to the block that day were all masked, so it was impossible to identify anyone. So, each witness was already contradicting the other. Furthermore, the prosecution's main witness had actually been initially arrested as a suspect but was later dismissed. Yet it was only after he'd been arrested that he'd named Sodiq, Qudus and David. So there were some key questions to be answered. Outside of his witness testimony, the prosecution had no other concrete evidence against these three boys – everything else was circumstantial.

Jordan, like me, had no concrete evidence against him, but the prosecution was trying to pin it on him anyway. The same went for the brothers who I did not know, for hiding the alleged, though not forensically proven, firearm.

Despite these holes in the prosecution case, and despite what I knew to be true, none of that information was going to save me today. After all the theatrics of the courtroom, I was starting to fear that the court is never interested in the actual truth, just who can tell their version of it better. What these twelve strangers on the jury believed would determine whether I would be sent down for a lifetime, or be walking home a free man. But the more airtime the prosecutor Penny had, the worse our chances of walking home felt.

And this was just day one. The prosecution had around three weeks more to present their case, and as far as I was concerned, this was too much time to poison the jury's mind. Could I bear any more days like this? Head bowed and looking down at my hands peeking out of the ends of my pristine white shirt, I felt defeated already. As I headed back to Feltham in the Serco bus, I'd lost any shred of hope I'd left prison with that morning. I replayed the courtroom scenes in my head. It was like watching a car crash that's about to happen but all I could do was fasten my seat belt and brace myself for the impact.

I didn't get back to Feltham till around 7 p.m. Throughout my whole trial I didn't arrive back until this time every weekday. From Monday to Friday, I was strip-searched every time I left and every time I came back from court. Ten times a week. Eventually I became numb to the whole process; it became part of my new normal.

My real issue, though, was that I often couldn't get a shower when I arrived back late at the prison. I would have thought that was my human right too, particularly after sweating my life away in a stuffy courtroom all day, but the prison would not accommodate me. Nobody seemed to give a damn about me or my hygiene. I was a prisoner, and I could smell like a garbage truck for all they cared.

So, I had to take matters into my own hands. Every morning, I got into the habit of having what inmates call a 'cell wash'. I would lay out a couple of the threadbare green bath towels on the floor and then strip naked, wet the soap under the tap and rub my body all over with it. Finally, I'd scrub myself and wash it all off using hot water from my sink.

Cell washes weren't ideal, but they were necessary. As with so much in prison, I had little choice.

As the weeks went on, the trial took its toll.

I could pretend to everyone else that I was okay and keeping strong, but I could not fool myself. There was a daily tug of war in my head between hope and hopelessness – and there could only be one winner. Hope would win the battle on most days, but hopelessness had a relentless spirit and would always come back fighting for the throne.

Some evenings after a rough day in court, I felt like a dead man walking. There were moments I wished I could hit my head up against a wall in my cell and just wake up out of this nightmare I was in.

I felt vulnerable. But being vulnerable wasn't me. I always saw being vulnerable as being weak. Growing up you couldn't be strong and be vulnerable at the same time. The two didn't mix, like alcohol and good decisions. Instead, I was schooled to be desensitized and removed from my emotions – and I was great at both. So, if I could feel this tsunami of emotions overpowering me, I knew that I was really broken.

I could see the burden of the trial playing out on my body too. Beforehand, I had started to grow one or two muscles and I was bulking up. But that all went down the drain. I didn't have time to go to the gym, and I lost my appetite. My clothes began to swallow me and started to look more like hand-me-downs from an older brother. I had lost a lot of weight in a flash.

One day, as I got into my cell after coming back from what had been a very tough day, I just dropped to my knees and prayed to God to rescue me. I couldn't bear to spend the rest of my life here. In prison I would read stories and psalms in my Bible about King David, the fearless, flawed, and strong man, who had killed a lion with his bare hands. There were countless Bible verses about how he used to cry out to God in his times of need. What I realized is that I had also become used to talking to God like one of my mates, yet I didn't cry out to Him. But this evening was different. I was exhausted, frustrated and in suffering. I pleaded with God to take me out of this situation and, as I did, my tears started to fall.

As the trial went on, the prosecution did their best to paint us as young, calculated, cold-blooded gangsters. The criminal records of some of my co-defendants gave him an open goal. When the jury learned that some of us had been found guilty of theft, assault, and being in possession of a knife, among other crimes, it didn't do us any favours.

If that wasn't bad enough, he then shared a You-Tube video that most of us, including myself, were in. The aim of showing the court the video was to prove that we knew each other, he said, even though we were never denying this at all. In fact, it was a very popular video, with hundreds of thousands of views – pretty rare for UK rap videos at the time. One of the opening lines to the song was one you definitely didn't want to hear in court. As the instrumental beat dropped I shrunk in my seat, knowing that before long all the jury would hear blasted out was: 'f**k da judge!'

This calculated move by the prosecution was just another nail hammered into our coffins. At this point I wouldn't blame the jury if they thought we could be the unruly savages and bunch of gang members and thugs that the prosecution was painting us out to be.

Penny was committed to sending us to a lifetime behind bars. He told the court about leaflets posted around the estate, warning:

No one likes a rat! Remember the police are not your friend.

Don't be deceived by promises of anonymity, protection and rewards.

They will say and do anything to make you snitch, then destroy your life. Be smart. Don't snitch.

This was all new to me. We had nothing to do with this at all, even if it was true. We later discovered that the flyers were part of Stop Snitching, a campaign against Operation Trident, the Metropolitan Police task force which investigates gun crime in London's Black communities. We had nothing to do with it. But the prosecution did not want to tell the jury that truth. Maybe because it wouldn't work in their favour. Or maybe the Trident officers didn't even tell him we were not connected; I wouldn't put it past them. But the implication was clear: we were going to such lengths to intimidate witnesses and obstruct justice.

But what really threw a spanner in the works during the prosecution's case happened only a couple of days in and it surprised us all. It was when the main witness, who their entire case relied upon, was called to give evidence.

The witness walked into the court, making no eye contact with anyone. Once he got inside the witness box, he spoke to take his oath and then sat down in silence – and remained silent throughout. He refused to answer any of Penny's questions.

All of us in the dock, as well as the jury, judge, Duncan Penny, and the whole court watched in disbelief. What was happening here? We were all here because of his witness statement, without it this trial would not be taking place. He couldn't just be silent now!

He wouldn't even speak to confirm his name, even after the judge warned him that a refusal to comply with his oath might amount to contempt of court.

He must have only been there because he legally had to be. Or maybe, and understandably, he was scared. Maybe his conscience was tormenting him?

My guess was as good as anyone else's at this point. The judge then concluded that the witness 'was determined to not cooperate in the slightest degree'. And asked him to leave.

Later, the prosecution made another attempt to question him. But the witness would only answer questions related to what happened before the incident. When Penny pressed him on more critical events, he resorted back to silence. Despite his reluctance, the one thing the prosecution got him to confirm was that he had told the truth to the police in his interviews. He said 'Yes.'

In the end, the prosecution claimed he was a hostile witness who should be dismissed, and this was argued out between both sides. While no one disputed that the witness was hostile, our legal teams argued that if he could not be openly questioned in court then his statements couldn't be openly challenged either. This would mean we would be deprived of the opportunity to cross-examine his account of the story. Instead, the jury would be relying on 'hearsay' evidence. Moreover, the witness was said to be a career criminal with a track record of lying in previous cases, so the merits of his testimony should be called into question.

Despite our genuine case to the judge that we would be disadvantaged if he allowed the prosecution's request, he still did so. This was a big blow for us. As if that wasn't bad enough, the judge also accepted another request by the prosecution to be able to replay relevant parts of the audio recording of the witness's significant police interview in the presence of the jury. He ruled that this would provide them with a better opportunity to assess the reliability and weight to be given to his evidence. But all this meant was that the jury would hear words he wasn't prepared to say in court – and there was nothing we could do to challenge those words. By this point, I concluded that the judge just didn't like us. He had heard the rap song and the shouts of 'f★★k da judge', and probably thought *well right back at you*. After that, everything the prosecution asked for they seemed to get.

When the witness was recalled to the witness box for the third time, and the recording was played to him, he sat with his head bowed. Then, without warning, he got up from the witness box and attempted to leave court.

He was just full of surprises. Even I was thinking, *where are you going?* He was in prison himself, on remand for another crime, so it's not as if he could do a runner. Eventually, police officers had to intervene to stop him. A violent struggle took place. Even the court security officers near where we were sat had to help restrain him and escort him from the court.

All of this happened right before the eyes of the jury, who were quickly led out while the courtroom calmed.

After that, lawyers working on our behalf applied for the whole jury to be dismissed. They could not forget what they had just seen and there was a danger they may discriminate against us because of the witness's behaviour. Predictably, the judge refused our application on the basis that he felt: 'the defendants' interests could be properly and adequately protected by firm directions from him.'

I was no legal expert, but I felt sure the judge had got this one wrong. People saw what they saw. They couldn't just be directed not to discriminate against us. The jury might interpret his actions as his conscience eating him up. They might think he was just an unreliable witness. Or they might think, after what they'd seen and heard in the rap video, or about the flyers or tales they knew about Peckham, that he really was scared. So scared of us that he refused to talk, and would rather be in contempt of court and even fight officers, than give evidence. If the jury thought this, then we were done for.

As far as I was concerned, we were losing. Penny had us on the ropes in this ring, swinging with his elite-school vocabulary and big-boy grammar. With unwavering conviction he painted a bleak, dangerous picture of us as Peckham Boys. He did not miss an opportunity to discredit us before we even shared our side of the story. The more he spoke, the more I despised him. By the end of the prosecution's case, looking at him made me feel physically sick.

When the prosecution's case came to an end on Tuesday 8 November, it was as if a weight had been lifted off me. Now we could begin the fightback. It was obvious there were gaping holes in the prosecution's case that we needed to exploit, and home truths we had to share. Up until now, the jury had only heard one side of the story. Surely they couldn't possibly hear our side and be so certain that we were guilty. But what did I know? Miscarriages of justice happen all the time.

But before we started the case for the defence, my legal team had an ace up their sleeves. They applied for what is known as a 'submission of no case to answer' – in other words they made an application to the judge saying there was no case to answer. Given the circumstantial and very limited evidence against me, alongside the jaw-dropping behaviour of the prosecution's main witness, my barristers argued that there were insufficient grounds to support a conviction, so the judge would have good reason to acquit me from all charges. It was a course of action that my barristers had been discussing beforehand. Now it was a reality, it could be the lifeline I needed.

As it turned out, the lawyers of six of us – all of us apart from Sodiq – applied for a submission of no case to answer. If any of us were successful, we wouldn't have to defend ourselves at all. We would be free men, and this would all be over – just like that. I could almost smell freedom and taste the sweet food of my mother's kitchen.

When I got back on to the wing that same evening, I had a fire of hope burning inside of me.

Even when I spoke to my mum on the prison phone, I told her that she should 'pray for me. Something in my spirit tells me I'm coming home tomorrow.'

Wednesday 9 November 2011

Simply saying this was a big day for me would be an understatement. I knew that if the judge did the right thing, which I was banking on despite his track record during the trial so far, it could be the last day I woke up in this miserable cell.

Today was also my last official day of being on remand, too, unless the judge extended it. But I didn't want to focus on that, I just wanted to go home.

Then, a bizarre thing happened. For months, I had been praying to God. The practice soothed me and helped me find peace in moments of intense stress, but I'd never felt Him speak back to me. I'd often heard my mother and people in the church talk about God speaking to them, but I'd never had that spiritual experience. Suddenly, in the quiet of my cell, I could hear God tell me something. He wasn't speaking to me, as such, but in my soul I heard Him loud and clear, as if He had placed these thoughts there.

The message was simple: I should pack up my stuff and write a note to give away my possessions, as I would no longer need them. What? To me, this seemed crazy. I sat there puzzled, trying to work it out. Who would pack their stuff into bags while halfway through a trial, unless they knew they were going home, or perhaps expecting to be sent to another prison after court?

Even my legal team, who had applied for a submission of no case to answer, had not told me to pack my stuff. I had no guarantee from anyone that I was going anywhere.

Nevertheless, it was the first time God had reached me like that so I knew to listen: I wrote a note and put it on top of my bed telling the prison staff on the wing to give away all of my snacks and toiletries to certain people, mainly those I knew who were doing long-term sentences, or were here for a while. And I packed away all my personal belongings.

I trusted God. The past six months in prison I had come to know Him in a way I had never known Him before. If I was being logical, my chances of going home were very slim, and yet suddenly I had an overwhelming confidence of this happening. It was far bigger than the actual odds. But I had now built a personal relationship with Jesus, and I knew that I could count on Him, in a way I couldn't even count on my best friends or parents. I knew that He would never abandon me, and would be with me all the way, whether I was given my freedom or not.

As I made my way to the Old Bailey that morning, another thought stirred in my spirit: *when you see David, Sodiq, Qudus and Jordan today, make sure you all pray together*. On the now familiar journey, I put it to the back of my mind. After all, we'd been together for weeks now and not prayed together, so why now? But the thought resurfaced not long after I got to court.

We were all placed in a holding cell together. I wanted to say: 'Let's pray together,' but then I had a doubt. Maybe that would be tempting fate? I couldn't live with myself if our prayer didn't come true.

Eventually, I gave in. 'Can we pray?' I asked. 'We need God's favour and mercy today.' To my surprise, everyone agreed and we stood in a circle and held each other's hands and prayed silently before we were escorted upstairs to the courtroom.

Just as we were on the stairs, a few floors up, an usher hurried down. 'You'll have to go back downstairs. The judge needs more time,' he said. With that, the court security officer led us back. My mind was going crazy. What was going on? Was this a good or a bad thing? Surely it was good? What were the odds of this happening right after we finished praying? God had intervened, I was sure.

With that confidence in my heart, I prayed even harder when I got back to the holding room. Soon, though, it was time to head back upstairs where the judge would be waiting. We all knew this was our deciding moment.

In the dock, I could feel my body starting to tremble and the sweat prickling on my skin. He explained he would now give his decision on whether an acquittal had been approved and for whom. Silence engulfed the room.

He called David's name, and asked him to stand. Looking straight at him he concluded: 'Request denied.' I almost felt David's body crumple even though I wasn't sat next to him. Then he moved along to Qudus. It was agonizing. I didn't want to hear the judge's conclusion. I thought if it was the same, things didn't look good for me. 'I will deny the request,' he repeated. My chest lurched forward in panic.

In that moment, I'd resigned myself to my fate. *Here he goes again,* I thought. Nothing goes in our favour with this judge. I stood bolt upright as soon as my name was called. If my heart pumped any faster, I would be on the verge of a heart attack.

This was the moment of truth . . .

Even now, I cannot recall what the judge said, word for word, but what I do know is that when he uttered the words: 'I have no choice but to ask the jury to acquit him of all charges,' my whole world changed.

Joy, gladness, relief, gratitude, hope, and every positive feeling you can think of enveloped me.

I was going home!

Can you flipping believe it?!

After all this heartache!

But within seconds those feelings were mixed with sadness, guilt and pain. I realized that I was facing the most bittersweet moment in my entire life. Jordan was up next. 'Request denied,' the judge said again. I couldn't help but feel guilty. As I was experiencing joy my co-defendants, most of whom were also friends, were still going to be on trial and could go down for thirty years. My nightmare was ending, but for them it could just be the beginning.

The only thing that made me hopeful was that in this joint enterprise case, I had been found not guilty by the judge. Surely this would mean the whole prosecution case falls apart? If we were all jointly responsible, as they claimed, and now one of us was out of the picture, then their story doesn't add up any more. So, my friends should be coming home too, right?

As I stretched my neck to look up into the gallery, I could see my mum and some of my friends smiling like Cheshire cats, beaming from ear to ear. They were overjoyed.

I told you, Mum! I thought.

On the other hand, Duncan Penny and the police officers certainly weren't smiling. They looked as though they could not believe the decision the judge had just come to. As I walked out of the Old Bailey and stepped on to the London pavement, I saw my mother right there waiting for me. I lifted up my arms to give her a big hug, like the old days when I was a child. I just stayed there in her arms, holding back the tears. That one minute I rested there in the warmth of her body, felt like a lifetime.

My mum had her handbag in one hand and McDonald's for me in the other. She had left the court and got it for me once she heard I was acquitted, but it was cold by the time I actually stepped out. But who cared, I was free!

11

Ashamed of My Own Name

'Every saint has a past, and every sinner has a future.'
— Oscar Wilde, *A Woman of No Importance*

'Kenny Imafidon.'

It's interesting that as a young boy I was ashamed of my name because I worried it sounded too African. Now I was ashamed of it for an altogether different reason.

Once I typed these two words into the Google search bar on my laptop, I knew that whatever flashed up could not be unseen. I sat alone in my mum's room, having not slept for over 24 hours since I walked free from court. Once I hit the enter button, I braced myself and watched the search results flood in . . .

'Fifth teenager charged over Peckham 17-year-old murder'

'Peckham murder trial case begins'

'Another charged in Peckham murder investigation'

'Teenager jailed for Peckham murder'

'A fifth teenager has been accused of murdering a 17-year-old athlete who was shot dead in south London.'

'Kenny Imafidon has been charged with murder, two counts of attempted murder and wounding with intent.'

Murder, violence, guns, gangs and Peckham. This was all my name had become associated with.

My mind was flooded with all sorts of questions:

How on earth could I move forward with my life?

How could I put all of this stuff behind me? Was that even possible?

How could I ever get a job?

What would people who I met think of me when they searched for my name on the internet, looking for my Facebook page, wanting to make friends, and stumbling across this instead?

How could I be expected to live my life normally, with all this information in the public domain for all to see, about me being in prison for murder? There were no articles saying I'd been acquitted. The news channels didn't seem interested in that side of the story.

And, was there a way I could get all these stories

written about me deleted now that I had been acquitted?

There was only one word that could describe how I felt and that was – to put it bluntly – FUCKED.

I had looked forward to various things when I got out: sleeping under my own bedcovers on a soft mattress; walking through busy crowds on London's streets; even just breathing fresh air that had circulated somewhere outside of prison – but this was not one of them. As long as this case was being talked about online or in the media, I would be forever on edge.

Then, something else would interrupt the sweetness of my homecoming – an unexpected phone call with my father.

He had rung my mum just as she, my stepdad, and I were making our way back home from Feltham to Peckham, in my stepdad's champagne-coloured seven-seater car. We had been there to collect my belongings, which I had packed to go with me to court. But there had been some mix-up at Feltham, and they hadn't brought them on the day I was acquitted. I was free, but my belongings were not. When I finally collected them, I found out that I was the only one out of all my friends who had actually packed their things, in crazy faith that I would be going home.

In the car, my dad exchanged small talk with Mum before she passed the phone over to me. This was the first time I had spoken with or heard from him in the whole 184 days I had been in custody. Up until this point, I had heard nothing – not even one letter. All he did was ask my mum for updates on me. He never booked one visit to come and see me, never sent me money or any other items I needed inside.

He never did anything. As usual.

But, look at that, the first day I was out and free, *now* he reappears.

'*Ób'àvàn*,' I said, wishing him a good afternoon, but without any real enthusiasm.

'Uhh hum, Kenny, we thank God that you're out now, I hope you are fine?' he replied in his monotone voice.

Before I could even answer, he continued without skipping a beat: 'But you have brought shame to this family name.'

SHAME!? I clenched my teeth, gripping the phone. Every fibre in my body wanted to hit back with some cutting comment, but I held back out of respect. I tuned out the rest of what he said to me. I was too stunned. How did he have the audacity to drop that on me like that?

This was the same man who did not contact me when I was going through the toughest period of my life. This was the same man who had been practically absent throughout my life. If anybody was to be ashamed, it should have been him.

As if I wasn't low enough, he thought it would be wise to kick me while I was down. What was it that the poet Maya Angelou said?

'People will forget what you said, people will forget what you did, but people will never forget how you made them feel.'

I couldn't remember a single thing he said in that conversation – with his consistent, even voice that never showed any emotions, no sense of love or care towards me – but I can never forget the anger, sadness and disbelief I felt. Once he had finished his shame speech, I passed the phone back to my mum without saying a word.

She did her best to comfort me. She could see how rocked I was by the conversation. I was fuming, and the tears that trickled down my cheek said it all. She had not seen me cry in a very long time.

At home, still blown away by my dad's comments, I sought refuge in my mum's den, also known as the living room. As usual, she hogged the space and the TV as if it was her own room. I sat down on my chair next to the sofa, quietly devastated.

I turned to Mum, glued to another of her Nollywood films.

'I need to change my surname,' I announced.

Immediately, she took her eyes off her film. I had her attention.

'Why would you do that?' she replied, shocked.

For me, there were many reasons. And as I let her know each one, I could feel the emotion rising in me.

'I do not want to bear the surname of a man like

my dad. How can he say that me, *me*, I'm bringing shame to the family? Does he know what I have just been through, and all he cares about is the family name?'

Once I began it was difficult to stop: 'He's just arrogant, no empathy, and to be honest, what's he ever really done for me anyway? Anything he has done, more times than not, me or you had to shout or beg for it. Seriously, if I am bringing shame to the family name then he can keep his surname.' It was a verbal torrent that I'd bottled up for so long, it became a tsunami.

My mum listened, but she was firm in her reply. 'Kenny you shouldn't do that, trust me,' she said.

Her response frustrated me. Why would she tell me that? This man hadn't done anything for her either, at least not in my lifetime. I'd assumed she would be happy about it. Why was she being so loyal? Did she still love him or something? Or was this just some African respect type of thing, and what I was telling her was a taboo? Because right then, I didn't give a damn. At that moment, I would have rather been called Kenny X than Kenny Imafidon.

'Just think about it, Kenny,' Mum continued. 'And don't make any rash decisions. But my advice would be to not change your surname.'

I rolled my eyes in annoyance. I just wanted her

agreement. I knew that night I wasn't going to get it, so I sighed and retreated to my room.

During my first few days of freedom, I had only been able to fulfil a handful of my plans. Top on the list had been sleeping soundly in my own bed. As for discovering London again, I had found it enough to be at home with family. That said, my phone kept blowing up. The news that I was out had spread like wildfire. People were happy that I was free, and calling constantly to give their 'fresh home' greetings. I appreciated the love, the warm welcomes, the kind gestures, and everything else that I had missed on the outside. But I had other things at the forefront of my mind.

Some of my friends were trying to get me to celebrate my freedom with them, but I wasn't comfortable with that. I was not in the mood to be going to a club, popping bottles, and living each night like it was my last. I may have been free but my co-defendants were still on trial and in the same hellhole I had left them in. I just couldn't. Until their nightmare was over, and they were free too, there would be no rejoicing for me. I felt we were all in it together – it wasn't just their trial, it was still mine too.

The hardest part of waiting for the day when they might be out was that I was advised not to come to court and show my support, in case it prejudiced the jury. Instead, I would have to make do with regular updates from their families and friends who attended court, or whenever one of my friends on trial called me with their own updates.

The most nerve-racking time, though, while waiting for our trial to finish was when the jury was out for deliberations. In that time, they would have to decide on the fate of each defendant. I ran over the scenarios in my head. Who would they believe was innocent or guilty, and on what charges? The jury could take anything from two minutes to two weeks to deliver their verdict. So, every day was a waiting game.

Though I knew I could not sit in the court's public gallery for the case I had just been acquitted from, I did come to the Old Bailey once, while our trial was still live. One of my close friends was a defendant in a separate trial there.

On the day, the line to get inside the court was almost as long as the overnight queue of customers waiting for the latest iPhone to go on sale in the West End. *Could it be for our trial?* I wondered as I looked up and down the line. I decided not – just too many people, and cameras, too. When I asked, it turned out everyone was there for the high-profile Stephen Lawrence murder case. *Wow*, I thought. *I am witnessing history*. If you are a Black boy in London, the name Stephen Lawrence is baked into your consciousness.

Stephen's parents had been tirelessly campaigning for justice for their son's murder, which happened on 22 April 1993 – about two weeks before I was even born.

Stephen was my age, eighteen years old, when he was stabbed to death in an unprovoked attack by a gang of White youths as he waited at a bus stop in Eltham, south-east London. On the day I was attending court, two of the alleged murderers, Gary Dobson and David Norris, were being retried following a review of forensic evidence.

The whole country was paying attention to how it went, particularly because the case had taken so long to get to this point, due to the police's catastrophic handling of it. That had led to the publication of the Macpherson Report in 1999, which concluded that the Metropolitan Police was institutionally racist. To me, that case was just another example of how Black people are treated in the system. Whether you were a victim, a victim's family or, like me, on trial for a crime you didn't commit, discrimination still exists.

It was mid-December when I woke up to a text from Sodiq's cousin Jide: the jury had come to a decision that morning, he wrote, and they would be sharing it later.

My heart was racing, and I wasn't even outside the court yet.

This was it.

The moment I had been waiting for in this eight-week trial.

I had been out for thirty-three days now, and I just wanted this nightmare to come to an end, once and for all. For all of us.

In all the time the trial had been ongoing I'd felt in limbo, desperate to move forward with my life, but I couldn't. It also kept alive the memory of everything that had happened to me. I just wanted to bury the experience so deep that I'd forget where I buried it. If that was even possible.

While I was hopeful that the jury would bring back not guilty verdicts for all defendants, I also knew that could be quite unlikely. However, I could not let myself entertain any of those dark, guilty-verdict thoughts. Bad energy was the last thing I needed to bring to the court that afternoon. It was strictly positive thinking and good vibes only.

As I waited outside, the jury inside courtroom 8 at the Old Bailey read aloud their verdicts:

Jordan: found not guilty of all charges.

Gabriel and Emmanuel: found not guilty of all charges.

Qudus: found not guilty of all charges.

David: found not guilty of possessing a firearm with intent to endanger life. However, he had a 'hung jury' – the jury could not agree on a verdict for his remaining charges, so it was likely he would be having a retrial.

Last but not least, Sodiq . . .

On the count of murder:

Guilty.

On the two counts of attempted murder:

Guilty.

On the two counts of grievous bodily harm:

Guilty.

On the count of possessing a firearm with intent to endanger life:

Guilty.

On the count of possessing an offensive weapon, namely a knife:

Guilty.

The minute I heard the news, my heart dropped to my feet. Grief consumed me.

Not Sodiq, I thought. He was only nineteen. I knew that if he was convicted for this murder, he would be getting a thirty-year life sentence. And that was a minimum. He would be serving a sentence longer than his current age. How can you comprehend thirty years when it is a decade longer than the life you have already known?

It was just insane. And so many questions were left unanswered: how could the jury be so sure it was him based on hearsay evidence from a witness that we didn't even get the chance to cross-examine?

Were they sure enough to put him away for thirty years?

I knew that Sylvester's family deserved justice, and rightly too. They were the true victims here. But I wondered, did the police and the prosecution care, truly, about who actually did it?

But it was too late now. The jury had already made up their minds. Sodiq was my brother. I couldn't stand to see him in this position. He would have to appeal but only God knew how long that would take. Also, his girlfriend had just given birth to their daughter before he came to prison. This innocent girl who was tiny enough to carry with one hand, would now have to grow up without her dad present, and not by his choosing either. His daughter could be married and have a child herself by the time he got out. A lot could happen in three decades, and a lot would.

Life would be for ever different for us, too. We wouldn't be able to create any new memories together. Sodiq had been robbed of any new experiences outside of the repetition of prison life. Our interactions would be limited to ten-minute telephone calls, and two-hour-long prison visits, where the journey to the prison could be longer than the time we spent together.

Yet, regardless of the circumstances, and Sodiq now being classed as a convicted murderer, I knew I would stick with him throughout this sentence no matter how long it took. Even if everybody deserted him, I would be one of a handful of people present in his life. If I were in his position – and I really could have been – I trust he would have done the same. I knew the world would forget him eventually – out of sight, out of mind. But I wouldn't. I'd make sure.

The trial may have been over, but the impact of it was just beginning. The news of Sodiq's conviction was all over the news in the UK, and even Nigeria. Everyone on the streets was talking about it too. No one in our age group who was well known from the ends had ever been convicted for such a major crime before, so it sent big shockwaves through everyone – that this stuff is for real. People were really getting them 'dirty thirties'. Sadly, though, this was never going to be a deterrent to stop people picking up guns or knives. Because people will for ever believe '*It'll never happen to me.*'

Now, more than ever, I felt like God had rescued me. So, I knew that I could not sit at home in a pity party, feeling sorry for Sodiq, and sorry for myself too. If I had any temptation to return to the streets, to selling weed, to stealing and violence, it had to end right here. I'd had big dreams before I went to prison of becoming great, though what that looked like I wasn't sure. But I damn sure knew it was far from the reality I was currently living. I couldn't let my life go to waste. I had to make something out of it.

But, guess what? I talked a good game and it all made sense in my head. Yet despite everything I told myself in prison, and when I got out, I still almost slipped.

The theory was much easier than the practice. There were only so many months I could keep going, not living the life I'd gotten accustomed to before I went to prison. I was addicted – to the status, to the power, and to the money. My withdrawal symptoms were strong. I wasn't enjoying my new status as the 'broke one' in my friendship group – I didn't tell anyone, but I knew, and that was all that mattered.

I needed more income so I had to hustle – well, this is what I convinced myself at least. And I relapsed. I had been in conversation with Femi, and as conversations can quickly go, we started talking about how we could make money, and soon settled on a new drugs business. A bad move, I know. And I am ashamed that I even entertained it. What idiot would risk their freedom again after a very close shave with the criminal justice system?

I am that idiot.

I was a creature of habit, and I could not help myself.

No matter how much I tried to suppress it, I was soon back to juggling a double life. Femi had a business phone that he gave me, and he drove me around to show me where some of the customers lived. Just like when I was younger and I needed money desperately, this was all I needed to hit the ground running. Things were slow in the beginning, but we had just started, so that was expected.

I was only a few days in, sitting in my living room eating my doner meat and chips from Perfect Fried Chicken, and the phone rang. It wasn't a customer though. It was my friend Mide.

'Yoooo, how you doing, bro?'

'Yooo, my brother from another mother! I'm blessed, how you keeping?' I replied, feeling glad to hear from him. Mide and I were close, and I considered him part of my inner circle.

'I am good, bro. What you on, man?'

'I'm just trying to get my bread up. I am back on the trap now still,' I told him. I said it casually, because I was still trying to downplay it to myself.

'Swear down?' Mide responded, sounding shocked. He was silent on the other end for a second. It caught me off-guard. Mide was also caught up in that lifestyle, but similar to me, he was trying to make something better of himself. The one-foot-in, one-foot-out type. If anyone got it, I thought it would be him. 'Bro, I can't lie, you got too much to lose,' he said.

Hearing Mide tell me this just hit me different. Maybe it was because I was so used to giving him words of wisdom, that when he gave me some – and he rarely ever did – I was taken by surprise. Mide wasn't even earning an honest living himself, but he cared enough to tell me the truth.

Mide didn't even know it, and I never told him either, but those few words he said to me changed my life. His statement was the straw that broke the camel's back and my relationship with the streets. There and then, I quit.

I also called up Femi straight away to let him know I was out for good. He understood. Besides, he was never going to force me or encourage me to do otherwise. Deep down, I think he was proud that I vowed to never again go into that type of business. And this time, I meant it.

Adapting to life outside of prison was a learning curve for me, and I knew I couldn't afford any more expensive lessons. I was lucky on that occasion that I quit while I was ahead, and did not return to the streets, but I also knew my luck could not last for ever. The temptation to make money by any means lingered but I never gave in. I knew that eventually I would be in jail – again – if I kept playing with fire. The only difference was that if I did end up inside this time, I couldn't expect sympathy from others. I would be single-handedly guilty of all charges. No one else to blame but myself.

Then I thought about Sodiq, who had just turned twenty when he'd been handed his sentence. He wouldn't be able to be released on parole until 9 February 2042.

2042.

What would the world even look like by then? Would there be flying cars? Would solar-powered planes be used for commercial flights? What would mobile phones be capable of? My young 18-year-old brain couldn't even comprehend life that far ahead. But the one thing I knew was that it was a very long time.

I didn't know where to start, but I knew that I had to get a move on somehow. Heading in some direction at least was better than standing still. Yet at the same time I just wanted to hide off-the-grid and be forgotten. I could have moved hundreds of miles up north to another city, or moved to the countryside to start life on a farm – probably not a farm, though, but the thought crossed my mind. I wanted to be forgotten about – uncontactable and untraceable to everyone but my immediate family.

I did not want my name to be coming out of people's mouths connected with the words murder, attempted murder, violence, guns or gangs. I had to be remembered for better things.

In the hood, all these associations would give

me credibility but in the real world none of this was anything to be proud of.

It was shameful.

But how could I live again with this type of reputation? I needed to build my life back up, but not in the way I had known it before. This operation was not going to be easy or straightforward. But nothing worth doing ever is.

It was now 2012. The year when the Olympic and Paralympic Summer Games were being hosted in London. Olympic fever was spreading and it felt contagious.

Now that I was on a de facto gap year from university, I had all this time on my hands and I needed to use it creatively. Travelling wasn't on my radar, but valuable work experience and volunteering were. And I knew the perfect person who could support me with both.

Jonathon Toy from Southwark Council was the one person I could count on to support me on my journey post-Feltham. I could trust him to give me a helping hand up off the floor, where life had thrown me. He wouldn't judge me like others, and he wouldn't judge me based on any news headlines. He'd seen and experienced a different side of me. He'd even seen a side to me that most of my friends had not. He saw my raw potential and my vulnerabilities, probably better than me. Jonathon had an ability to look past all my wrongdoings, poor decisions, and the questionable characters I was surrounded by, to support me.

And he had promised me when I was in Feltham that he would support me when I was out. So, I took him at his word.

I still had Jonathon's number in my makeshift phone book – a pocket-size calendar I scribbled on in prison to store key people's contacts. I punched his eleven digits into my BlackBerry phone, and pressed call.

The phone rang twice and then I heard the words: 'Jonathon Toy speaking,' always sounding as formal as a corporate receptionist.

'Hi, Jonathon, it's Kenny Imafidon, how are you doing?' I cheerfully replied.

'How are you? – that's the real question . . .' he shot back, but with genuine concern in his voice. This was not our first conversation since I had come out, but it was the first since Sodiq had been found guilty.

'I'm all right, you know,' I lied. I was far from it. We talked briefly about how Sodiq and his family were bearing up, before I hit him with my request.

'I need your help with some sort of paid work experience or internship. Like what I did with you before but longer, as I won't be going to university any time soon,' I told him.

He didn't even hesitate. 'No worries, just leave

that with me, I will speak with some people and come back to you,' he replied. This was music to my ears, and exactly what I needed to hear.

'Thank you, Jonathon, I really appreciate it,' I told him.

My conversation with Jonathon left me feeling optimistic for the future and whatever was coming next. I was very lucky to have people like him in my life, who were part of my support system. Unlike me, a lot of people who leave prison have no strong support system or people championing them. But Jonathon did what he had always done. He went above and beyond to make things happen for me. Being a man of his word, he provided me with more than just mentorship, but practical and financial support too, the two keys I needed to open the door to success.

Not long after my call, Jonathon secured me an internship with a consultancy firm who advised on and delivered capacity-building services to local authorities and community-based organizations. I worked under a half-Jamaican, half-Cuban man called Viv, a Windrush baby born in the sixties. He was a strategic thinker and a sort of community activist, a guy who took his fitness seriously. He and I got on well; it was like having an uncle at work. The internship put £100 a week in my pocket, ten times what I had been making doing the kitchen job at Feltham, but nothing compared to what I had been earning on the streets. But it was while doing this internship that my prayer was finally answered – the creative idea I was seeking came to me.

There wasn't a eureka or lightbulb moment, but the desire came out of nowhere.

I wanted to write a report.

I had experienced first-hand the street life and social challenges that many of these academics in the criminology and sociology space wrote about but had never lived themselves. So, I wanted to share a different story. I wanted to contribute to the discussion about how we can solve this major issue traumatizing our society and, even more so, the people who grow up in communities where crime is an ever-present issue.

In this report I wanted to answer the big questions about how we solve this 'gang problem' in our society, because the justice system is clearly not deterring gangs and serious youth violence.

I also wanted to include a detailed case study that painted a real picture, unlike anything seen before. A picture that shows how many young people from areas like Peckham are on the edge of being involved in gangs every day, or are simply just opportunists who get lured in for money. Some young people feel they have no choice. And for others it's just a matter of survival and safety. If anything, given the circumstances, it's a miracle we have so many young people from deprived areas who are not involved in crime.

I knew my report wouldn't be the first, as there had been many inquiries, investigations, and research papers attempting to answer this question, but not enough progress had been made. Surely a report from an author with a real lived experience would add something different to the conversation? I had a real bugbear when it came to the lack of understanding about, and stereotyping of, people from communities like mine: that all Black boys who wore hoodies were a threat and were 'uncouth' and violent, and the reason we were poor was because we were lazy, wasting time in gangs rather than making a proper living.

I understood more than most how people could be quick to judge others harshly about the choices they made, with no understanding of their context. Just like the politicians I'd been so frustrated by in Parliament, many of these people had not walked even a metre in our shoes, let alone a mile. And if they were faced with the decisions many young people in Peckham faced, they might, to their surprise, have made the same decisions. It's always interesting how people are very good lawyers when it comes to their own mistakes but very good judges about the mistakes of others. We judge ourselves by our intentions and others by their behaviours.

I came to several conclusions, drawn from my

own life: the 'lock up all these criminals and throw away the key' stance we have in the UK needs to be challenged. It is clearly not working. Our prison population has risen by 70 per cent in the last thirty years – and is currently projected to rise by a further 18,000 people by 2026.[1] The longer sentences that some call for, as well as the politicized nature of being tough on crime, are not paying dividends for our society. In my report, there was a fact I returned to and still do today: that England, Wales and Scotland have the highest imprisonment rates in Western Europe. And the number of people sentenced to twenty years or more has quadrupled in the last decade.[2] Still, we are not solving this issue.

Sentences for more serious crimes have also been getting longer, with many more people spending periods in prison which would have previously been unimaginable.[3] One of the biggest issues I've seen is that there are endless discussions about criminal justice in politics, yet when I entered the political space I was frustrated by the inaction and lack of leadership. There has been no real change to people's realities, despite all the talk. I needed to see the change we all deserved. My hope was that this report would help nudge things forward or at least make some noise and ruffle some feathers.

I spent a little more time making sense of what I wanted to do, working with Viv and Junior at the consultancy firm I was interning at to help me develop my ideas. Once I felt like I had something really concrete, one of the first people I rang was Jonathon.

'Jonathon, how are you doing? And do you have a few minutes please?'

'Of course, I always have time for you,' he replied.

I dived straight into my big pitch like a door-to-door salesman. 'So, Jonathon, I need your help with an idea. I have been thinking about it for a while now. I want to write a report,' I said, reminding him of his report on reducing youth violence and knife crime and how impactful it had been. 'Mine will be on a different topic. Hopefully as impactful. Can I tell you about it?' I waited anxiously for his reply. I wasn't too sure how he would receive it all.

'This sounds amazing, tell me more,' he replied excitedly.

'So yeah, I want to write a report that looks into the socio-economic factors that lead young people into crime and violent lifestyles,' I said, feeding off his enthusiasm. 'I want to paint a real picture. How many young people from areas like mine are on the edge, daily, of being involved in drugs, crime and gang violence. I don't want this to be some dry rubbish. I want to talk to people. My people. People who have been in prison, people who are currently committing crime, people who live in high-crime areas, even politicians, police officers and lawyers. I want a 360°-picture on the problem. I want to interview everyone.'

After ten minutes of listening to my own voice, I even convinced myself this report would be unlike anything the political world had seen before.

'This report can help everyone get a better understanding of the challenges, issues and complex needs facing our communities, and the lives of young people in these high-crime areas. But most importantly it will also provide practical solutions too.'

'Kenny, this sounds brilliant!' Jonathon said, sounding even more excited. 'I will definitely support you with this.'

I thanked Jonathon, and I was just about to hang up when I realized I had one more very important ask. I knew that the answer would determine whether my report went ahead or not. 'I'll need some funding to do this. I have no money and I want to do this full-time to keep me busy until I start university, which is like a good nine months from now. So, something to cover my expenses and stuff would be very much appreciated.'

'I see, I see,' Jonathon said. 'Let me see what I can do. But all of this sounds amazing.' He spoke to me like a proud uncle.

The call had ended but the ideas pinballing around my mind had only just begun.

12

It Pays to Be Yourself

'If you don't know who you are at 9 a.m., by dinnertime someone's going to tell you who you are.'
– John Hope Bryant, *The Memo*

If I was ever to be convicted of an offence in this life, it would have to be for the crime of living a lie. I was guilty of spending most of a decade denying who I was deep down – the person I was raised to be. The pressure of being an overachiever throughout my school life while also maintaining my reputation on the streets, meant I had to carefully, and at times recklessly, juggle these identities with conflicting priorities.

No one ever really knew the real Kenny. No one ever got to know the man behind either mask. Even I didn't know who I was, so what chance did anyone else stand? I had been trying to build a

Lamborghini life with a Ford KA engine. It didn't make any sense.

I didn't want to look under my bonnet either. Maybe I was afraid of what I might see, or maybe I enjoyed the bliss of my ignorance. I comfortably preferred to create and live up to an image of the person I was in my head. So, I didn't make any time to get to know who I was on the inside – underneath all this eye-catching bodywork, of course.

Only by knowing who you are can you be a truly authentic person. To be authentic means to be 'genuine' and 'not a copy'. Being authentic basically means to be 'real'. It means to be consistent about who you are in both public and private settings.

If I didn't grasp a lot of this after I left prison, I wouldn't have been able to work on my first research project. Jonathon had given me the opportunity of a lifetime and secured pay of £100 a week, mainly to cover my living expenses, but it certainly wasn't a pay rise. Based on what I was earning from doing 'odd jobs' in Peckham before, £100 was peanuts. From now on life would have to be about strict budgeting and making my pay packet stretch. It was like going back to square one all over again. But I ate my humble pie.

When I thought about it, I was back to being in the financial position I had been in before I sat in Gloria's place and saw the black dustbin bags lying on the floor in the middle of the room, filled with half a kilo of weed. That day was the beginning of a financial turning point for me, and so was the day I got the call from Jonathon telling me he had secured an extra £50 a week for me to help me with my report. That meant I would be living on £150 a week while I worked on it.

It wasn't very much, but who was I to complain? And I probably sound ungrateful, but I wasn't. I knew this was a once-in-a-lifetime opportunity to do something I was passionate about, something I could be proud of.

More importantly, I needed to live a life on the straight and narrow, and be broke too, if I had to. I couldn't afford new designer clothes but more than that, I couldn't afford to go back to prison. This was just my new reality and I had to embrace it. I had to learn to be content with where I was right now and who I was becoming. Prison must have taught me something, right?

Every day I had to remind myself of how blessed I was to have my freedom and how I couldn't waste it. Several weeks after Jonathon rang me to tell me his good news, I woke up to find that David had not found favour with the jury in his retrial. After what happened to Sodiq I couldn't be too shocked any more. Also, I was emotionally numb to it all by this point. I had no words. The jury found David guilty of murder. The judge sentenced him to a minimum of twenty-six years. That's a minimum of 9,496 days in prison. Learning this knocked the wind out of me and was heartbreaking. I knew a guilty verdict was a very real possibility, but it still hit me.

In the months between my release and David's retrial, my relationship with him had really developed. I got to know him more deeply in our phone calls and when I visited him than I had before. So, I felt his pain.

I could have been him or Sodiq. I could have been the one with a life sentence of thirty years, or twenty-six years. And they could have been me too. Every time I sat opposite them in the visitor hall on a prison visit, I knew that the only thing separating us was a decision by a jury and a judge. And I could easily have been sitting on the other side.

It was for these guys, and my brothers who I grew up with in the hood, that I felt so compelled to write the report. I needed the world to know that we were more than just statistics, that we had been set up for failure by systems not designed to support us. Though we all have to accept personal responsibility for our decisions, the choices seemed limited from where we were standing. But I couldn't do it all by myself. I was new to the process of what it takes to write a report.

I needed support. I needed a community.

Firstly, Jonathon said he knew just the person to put me in touch with.

'He is one of the country's top criminologists and is well respected. His name is Professor John Pitts, have you met him before?' he enquired.

'No, I haven't. But I'll look him up,' I promised.

'Yes, do, and read his book too. I will try and set up a meeting. Leave it with me.'

When I googled him, I learned he was a professor of both socio-legal studies and criminology, and his book was an in-depth study into gangs in east London. He was the guy who would show me the ropes of how to structure and write a research paper, and he acted as a sounding board for all of my ideas.

Viv and Junior at the consultancy firm were also useful sounding boards, who I could work-shop ideas with. Then there was a headteacher friend who had worked in a school in the Gambia called Aunty Pat, who reviewed and proofread my work, alongside a middle-aged White lady called Dinah. Dinah was trained in hypnotherapy and counselling, and she was all into psychotherapy. She also gave me constant feedback on drafts of my work (when she wasn't trying to give me therapy). And there was Gwenton, too, a reformed roadman himself, originally from Jamaica, and an ex-convict. He offered me a space in his office in

Hackney to write from when I did not want to write at home.

Whoever first said teamwork makes the dream work didn't lie. All of these people and more played their part on the journey, including the fifteen-plus people I began to interview for my research. I had no name for the report until Viv suggested one day to name it 'The Kenny Report' and I thought on reflection, *do you know what, that name sounds good.* And that was that. The Kenny Report was the name we went with moving forwards.

However, even with my report becoming a reality, it was still a gap year project, something for me to do to keep myself occupied. The elephant in the room was what would happen to my life after. I had not vowed to become the first person to sit A levels in Feltham for no reason. I wanted to secure a university place.

But with the tragic grades — at least to me — that I had got, I would not be able to go to any of my preferred university choices. I'd probably have to go to some hillbilly university that took anyone who was paying. Another, less desired option, was to spend an extra year doing what they called a foundation course, or access course, to attend a top-tier university. But this would also mean graduating two years later than my friends who I had finished college with.

I didn't want to do that either.

I was already behind enough as it was.

Plus, I was still feeling the symptoms of being in prison, and desperately wanting to catch up on lost time. I was in a rush to get my life in order – nobody else was going to do it for me. But I was luckier than most. Many prisoners leave jail without stable accommodation to go to and end up squatting, sofa-surfing or even being homeless. Without accommodation people can't access a discharge grant, which at the time of writing is £76 given to people for their first few days of life on the outside.[1] They can't access ongoing benefits, either. And, around 17 per cent of people who leave don't find a job within a year of them being free.[2] Even if people want to get on with their lives, the system is stacked against them. I was lucky to have my mum's to go back to, and I was not going to waste a minute of my freedom – I needed to get my life on track. Colin had told me, back in church, that God would recompense me for the lost time, but I wasn't just going to sit on my hands and wait for Him either.

I had spent half a year of my life in custody, and I had not received any form of compensation from the police or the Crown Prosecution Service. Not one penny to make up for the irreplaceable time that I had lost in prison and all the emotional distress caused. Not even a simple sorry, even an acknowledgement. Again, this is the case for so many people. In fact, prisoners can only be recompensed for a wrongful conviction and, even then, there is no guarantee a person will receive this. The same is true for an ex gratia payment sometimes awarded by the Home Office for time wrongly spent in custody, but it is only granted in exceptional circumstances.

What really bugged me most though was not even the extra year I would have to spend if I wanted to go to a respectable university, but that the cost of going to university had now tripled to £9,000 a year. Because I was in prison, I'd just missed the last cohort of undergraduate students who could pay the annual fees of £3,000. Consequently, my student debt would now be three times the amount it would have been if I had never been remanded and had gone to university as planned. Then, if I added the extra £9,000 that I would have to pay if I took a foundation year, it was like adding insult to injury.

It was a tough pill to swallow, and one I didn't want to either, but halfway through writing The Kenny Report a golden opportunity did come my way. By this point I had stopped resisting having to do an extra year, and was preparing to study a four-year degree which included a foundation year. I had also secured my part of a housing deposit to share a flat with my friend James and his friend Bilal, and despite having to do an extra year of study I was happy that I was moving towards something positive.

It was August 2012, and I had not too long ago finished a gym session with Viv. Viv was a gym junkie, and he didn't let his old – or should I say mature – age hold him back. He took pride in his fitness. This was my first time going to the gym with him, and we sat afterwards in the Pret by Vauxhall Bridge, he drinking a coffee and I a hot chocolate as usual – I refused to get hooked on any drugs, including caffeine.

'Did you see my email, son?' Viv asked. 'I popped you something over last night.'

'Let me check it now,' I replied, scrolling through my BlackBerry.

I read the email title aloud: 'Scholarships to study Law or Business: Deadline for applications 13 August 2012.'

'Yes, that is the one,' Viv said.

I went on to read the rest of the email, which had been forwarded to Viv by a contact who had received the original email from the Labour MP for Hackney North and Stoke Newington, Diane Abbott. An organization called the Amos Bursary was offering the chance for three students under the age of twenty to win a full three-year scholarship to study law or business at undergraduate level. Immediately, three things crossed my mind: firstly, law was not something I was particularly keen on studying, but I wasn't absolutely against it either. As for business studies, I definitely did not want to study that. After all, I'd proved I was pretty good at business (even if it wasn't legit), so why did I need to study it? Besides, most of the teachers wouldn't even have that hands-on experience.

Secondly, I thought, a scholarship? What chance did I have of getting a fully funded scholarship to study at one of the UK's top private universities? I was from the hood! Seeing people around here getting scholarships was as common as seeing snow in Nigeria. Lastly, but most importantly I thought, I didn't have the BBB A level grades required for the scholarship.

Yet Viv was convinced I had a good chance.

'You have other things that you bring that are more important,' he said. 'You can tell them about your background, what happened in your life, and your determination to do your A levels in Feltham. You have a compelling story, son.'

Viv was far more confident than me about my chances, and admittedly his confidence was infectious.

'But I don't want to study law,' I told him. I had always thought that when I did go to university I would study philosophy, politics and economics.

Viv's response was classic.

'Right,' he said. 'But do you have £9,000 a year for uni fees?'

'No, I don't,' I replied, knowing that was obvious.

'Well there's nothing to really talk about, is there? Unless you have the money to pay yourself. Law is a great subject and will give you a good grounding. A lot of people who have entered politics have studied it too,' he concluded.

But it wasn't that simple for me. Not that long ago, I had been in the courts fighting for my freedom. I had seen enough of lawyers and judges for my lifetime. The whole experience had left a bitter taste in my mouth. Maybe if I had never been arrested for this murder and experienced all that I did, I would have considered it. After all, I did like a good debate, and people did joke that I could make a good lawyer. But the thought of being back in the courts didn't sit right with me. I didn't have the heart to defend people who were very likely to be guilty, but neither did I have the heart to prosecute people who I thought were innocent – all in the name of doing my job. Obviously, there are many areas of law, from family law to corporate law and civil law, but none of these areas interested me like criminal and human rights law would.

If I were a lawyer, I thought, I would want to protect and fight for those wrongly accused, or those maliciously targeted by the police. But I feared I was too emotionally charged to be objective enough to do that job. How could I sleep at night if one of the people I represented got a thirty-year sentence? Probably, I would have experienced first-hand the lives of the people I represented. Maybe I would be too invested in those people? Would this be a weakness or strength for me? I didn't know. I saw purpose in being a lawyer but I just didn't think it could be me.

I didn't want to go back and forth with Viv. I heard him loud and clear and I did see where he was coming from. In the end, I reassured him: 'I will apply for this.'

Viv had done a good job of convincing me that the scholarship could be the golden ticket I had been waiting for. But I would need God to move heaven and earth to make this happen. I did not meet the requirements to apply for the scholarship, but I was prepared to give my all.

I only had one shot at this, and I needed to score.

This was the most audacious thing I had ever done.

It turned out Viv was right. Soon enough, I was walking past the Barbican, on a clear bright day, ready to attend my interview for the Amos Bursary. In a black Ralph Lauren polo and black trousers, I had dressed for comfort more than anything else, and I knew I looked good.

The scholarship interview took place at Linklaters, a 'Magic Circle' law firm, so called because they and a select group of others outperform the rest of London's law firms when it comes to profitability. Any person in their right mind attending an interview at Linklaters would have turned up in a suit. Not me though. I wanted to come as myself.

When I sat down opposite my interviewers, I disguised any feelings of nerves behind my strong smile. I knew that whatever questions they threw at me, I would be able to answer confidently, or at least make a good attempt to. Besides, Aunty Pat had prepared me with mock interviews, so that I felt ready. As we started, I could tell by the raised eyebrows and nodding heads that I was doing well. I was not pretending to be someone I wasn't. Either they wanted me or they didn't.

I also had a confidence that what I was doing with my report was going to make me stand out. It had taken nine months to take the report from just an idea to something that you could hold in your hand. We were due to be launching it in Parliament soon, and this alone made me sound impressive.

My interviewers were particularly impressed with the length of it. I was only nineteen, but had written the equivalent of a thesis for a Master's degree. If they were ever concerned that my grades might be a sign I couldn't handle the academic requirements of the course, the report was perfect proof to show otherwise. I sat a little more comfily in my chair, and waited eagerly for the next question.

'Why do you think you're worth a £30,000 investment?' one said.

For a split second, my mind went blank. That was a question I had not prepared for. It was hard, and definitely threw me off. After a pause, I made my case, but it wasn't easy.

'I may not have the grades, but I am determined,' I told them. I went on to talk about being the first person in Feltham to take my A levels, and how hard I had studied. And that the only reason that I could write my report was because I had been motivated and sought out work experience when I was at college, and created a network of people to support me.

When I left the interview room, I didn't know whether my speech would be enough, but I hoped the panel could see how dedicated I was.

A few days later my mobile rang.

'Kenny, we'd like to offer you the scholarship,' the voice on the other end said. *What?* I couldn't quite take it in, but I listened hard as one of the interviewers went on to explain that a condition was attached to the offer.

'Yours is not a standard route to join the Amos Bursary and secure this scholarship, but we were very impressed by you,' she said. 'For that reason, the requirement is that you pass a three-month access course to enter university. Do think about it, Kenny, and let us know your answer.'

I was still in shock from the offer. Really? Me? A bursary? After everything I'd been through. I was speechless.

As soon as I put the phone down I ran to tell my mum and stepdad, whose faces lit up with excitement. Then I rang Aunty Pat and left her a message to call me. That evening, just as she was about to board a plane, she rang from the airport.

'Well done, Kenny. I am so proud of you. Take it. Do the access course and take the scholarship,' she advised, and I knew in my heart that she was right.

Now it was my turn. The moment I had been waiting for, and I knew I had to deliver. Just 370 days earlier, I was standing trial, facing thirty years in prison for a murder I didn't commit. But on Tuesday 13 November 2012, my life looked very different. That day, I was in the House of Commons, wearing a black suit and blood-red tie, about to launch The Kenny Report to a roomful of friends, family, politicians, and influential people.

This was my new chapter.

We had been planning the event for months. And presenting a talk in such a venue is no easy feat. To present in the House of Commons I needed to secure a sponsor. Mine was Simon Hughes. At the time, he was the MP for Bermondsey and Old Southwark which was the area next to mine, the reason why I hit him up. He didn't know me from anywhere, he wasn't one of the connections I'd made throughout any of my various work experiences. I just sent a personalized email to his office and had to trust that his staff would pass on the message. We had a hit list of prominent politicians that we wanted to engage, and thankfully Simon was the first to be sold by the idea.

Once we had found Simon as our sponsor for the room – the Boothroyd Room in Portcullis House – we went about inviting our guests. We wanted to make sure it was a diverse group of people, from other MPs to members of the public – and, of course, I invited my interviewers from the Amos Bursary who had so kindly awarded me my scholarship and got me my place at university. On the day, I spotted my mum, stepdad, and little brother George, at the back taking it all in. Colin and Chris, prison chaplains from Feltham, were just in front of them too. The last time I had seen them I was living in cell 8 on Teal wing. I could also see some of my friends from the hood, college, and from secondary school.

Just like Tupac, all eyes were on me.

As I watched more guests trickle into the room,

I couldn't help but feel pride at what I'd achieved. This 28,000-word research study was written by someone who just about got his A levels in prison. It aimed to bridge the gap in knowledge of those who had no real insight into what it was like growing up in a violent and traumatized community.

Through my report, I wanted people to gain a deeper understanding of the real people involved in criminal lifestyles, not just provide insight into gangs as a whole. I wanted to shine a light on how the socio-economic issues that affect young people growing up impact their lives. I truly believe that only when we understand the relationship between socio-economic factors, individual responsibility, societal responsibility and criminality, particularly in deprived communities, can we get to the heart of the problem and make the right changes. It is not possible to solve a problem you do not fully understand, neither can you find solutions when political point-scoring ignores important facts, evidence and lived experience.

As well as people from all different walks of life who I interviewed, The Kenny Report also included a highly detailed case study of a guy called Harro, who had sadly died. While he was alive, society would have pigeonholed him as a gang member and a cold-hearted villain. Yet he could equally be described by his friends and family as a decent person with good manners and a heart of gold. He was a complex individual, but ordinary, too. By including him, I wanted to explore how various socio-economic factors impacted his life opportunities and outcomes.

Harro was a young man full of potential, who would still be alive today if the support he needed had been in place when he needed it, and perhaps also if he had made different choices. Although he was one individual, he shared so many characteristics with other young people involved in gangs, or those at risk of joining them. To delve deeper into the story of Harro, I'd divided my research up into seven significant themes: education, employment prospects, positive role models, housing, health, relationships and socialization, and community support. I found that a lack of any one of these things, or a combination, can affect young men like Harro, and can steer them in the direction of gang membership and committing serious youth violence. If attention and resources are given to them, these can equally steer someone away from it.

Now it was time to tell the whole room about my report. I stood up and puffed out my chest confidently, even though I could feel the force of gravity on my knees. I was nervous and my throat began drying up before I had even uttered a word. The last time I was this nervous I was sitting as a defendant in the Old Bailey. But I had to remind myself that I was here, in the Houses of Parliament, in a room crammed with over 130 people.

I quickly grabbed my cup of water and gulped it down. And when I looked up, I could see everyone patiently waiting for me to speak. I had no notes in front of me. Instead, this was a speech that I had been working on in my heart and in my mind for ages. This was my version of Dr Martin Luther King Jr's 'I Have a Dream' speech, coming live and direct from a Peckham Boy.

In that moment, I knew I had that dream for sure, that one day boys and girls from Peckham would have equal opportunities to succeed in life and live in a community they could take pride in.

'I know the saying well, "you don't have to be a product of your environment", but I felt like living proof,' I told the crowd.

I went on to explain that I had realized on this journey that by saying I was just 'a product of my environment' was a comforting belief I had adopted. It had stopped me from taking any accountability for my choices. And I simply used it as an excuse for my lack of agency, my lack of belief in my power and ability to get things done, and determine my own destiny.

'I know that many things influence or play a part in shaping us into who we are: our upbringing, our schooling, our gender, our ethnicity, our social class, our local community, and our parents.

However, we are all also blessed with the ultimate gift of life: choice. Where we are right now today is because of choices we've made in the past – or those made for us, which we had no control over,' I continued.

By saying that, I was not minimizing the tragic or unfortunate experiences faced by people in life. Many will not have had a choice about what they've experienced. But I was saying that despite what has happened, what happens – or does not happen – to you, you have a choice in deciding who you are going to be today. I also talked about how our environments can make us feel like we have a low sense of agency and not much choice. There are bigger structural and societal factors at play such as racism, sexism, poverty and more. Yet we are all also products of our choices and not just our environments.

'I had a choice: to be Kenny the Peckham Boy, which I craved, or Kenny the golden child that my mother raised me to be. What I lacked was agency. I was so used to a narrative being painted about me, that I fell into it without even realizing. When you have low self-esteem you're less likely to feel that you are in control of your life, and less likely to take responsibility for your choices. It took me a while to realize I had control over my own decisions,' I explained.

Suddenly, I looked out at the room, at people

listening intently to what I had to say. And I could hear my inner voice telling me something: *I do not have to be who the world told me I should be.*

Now, for every story you show me of someone who was a so-called 'product of their environment', I can show you another person in the same circumstances who turned out completely differently. If I turned a spotlight on myself, everything I did when I was younger, despite my difficult and volatile environment, was still a choice. I didn't talk about my drug dealing in my speech, but the truth of my story was at the front of my mind all the time. Growing up in a poverty-stricken community, with other poor families, I had a choice about how I would make a living. I made the choice to sell weed and make illegal money, not proudly, but it was what it was. Others chose to get a job, even if it was low-paying and they would just remain broke, temporarily at least.

I could argue that those who took the legitimate route never made more money than me. My choice was made for financial reasons. I was tired of lacking things I felt I needed or wanted. However, my peers growing up in the same circumstances and facing the same pressures, took alternative choices that were more positive, and arguably more profitable later on. I risked my freedom by making decisions that could land me in jail, while they were risking nothing by comparison. Looking back, I had a low sense of agency. Although I believed I was different, I played into the stereotypical narrative of being a Peckham Boy.

'On this journey of putting together The Kenny Report, I learned to take responsibility for my choices and that has shaped me into who I am today,' I told the crowd.

I had begun a journey of self-discovery. I had begun to realize more about who I was, and things that I wanted to address, even if reluctantly, such as throwing away all the excuses under the sun that I took comfort in.

I had to make a choice to raise my standards and become the person I wanted to be: more kind, more loving, more forgiving, more empathetic, less selfish, less egotistic. It really wasn't too late.

Holding the report up in my hand, I couldn't help but think to myself: this is what it feels like to turn your dream into a reality. There is no better feeling. And I had made it happen.

Of course, I also acknowledged that I could not have done this alone. During the process I had help along the way, a community and teamwork. I had people like Jonathon and Viv, and so many others, including my family. To anyone wanting to change their circumstances, like me, I say ask yourself three questions: who are you? Who do you want to be? And who is in your team – who are those people who are going to help you get to that next level and ensure that you fulfil your full potential?

I spoke about all of this in my talk, and ended up speaking for over seven minutes. There was absolute silence throughout, and when I reached the end, my inner voice spoke to me again: *I've done it*, I thought. But at that moment I was even more surprised. Immediately, people started clapping. Others joined and then a few stood up. More followed until the whole room was on its feet. For the first time in my life, I felt like a star in my own show – a theatre performance with a standing ovation.

The clapping went on for way longer than I thought it should have, and at points I felt very humbled. At the end of the event, someone from the Amos Bursary scholarship even marched over to shake my hand. When I looked up and saw Viv, he nodded at me and gave me a thumbs up.

Who, including myself, could have ever foreseen this moment? I could not have written it. Going from the most traumatic experience in my life, standing in the defendant's box in the highest court in the country, to standing in a room in a world-famous government building, where I was being showered with compliments and applause. The choices I had made since leaving prison had got me to this point. What happened to me, and what didn't happen to me, changed me for the better, and in unexplainable ways too.

The 18-year-old Kenny who spent 184 days of his life in prison didn't see this coming. But here I was, applause rippling over me. Yet among the handshakes and the congratulations and the sheer pride of getting there, there's one moment from that day seared into my memory. I took a moment to look over at my stepdad and Mum and my brother George, clapping just as proudly. They were smiling and I smiled back at them. Then I thought about George. I was his positive role model now, not the brother he had visited in prison. I knew now I had so much to learn myself, but also to teach him. This was just the beginning of greater things to come, and our best days were still ahead of us.

13

Fast Forward to the Present

'We always overestimate the change that will occur in the next two years and underestimate the change that will occur in the next ten.' – Bill Gates, *The Road Ahead*

It is now more than ten years since I was on remand for a murder I didn't commit. Revisiting this past has not always been comfortable, but I set out to give readers an unfiltered insight into my life. I was a Peckham Boy – two words that meant crime, violence, poverty and hopelessness. Today, I am still that Peckham Boy, but those words have a different meaning. Now, they represent progress, success, joy and fulfilment. I am living proof that no one is a product of their environment. We can all learn, grow and change.

My life has changed drastically in the last decade. From the mess I was in, I have rebuilt it step by step through making different choices. I have a deeper understanding of who I am and who I want to be. On my journey, I've learned that it's not about how high you can go, but how deeply you can understand yourself. I have come to see God's favour, and I am extremely grateful for all He has blessed me with – a second chance at life.

I've learned that there is no shortcut to success. No matter what people promise, you cannot take the elevator. You must take the stairs. The journey ahead may look like a thousand miles, but it all starts with one step. My first step started all those years ago with my work experience at City Hall. Now, I am a graduate in law and a proud recipient of the Amos Bursary. I've been a trustee of the British Youth Council and have represented the views of over seven million young people to national and international governments. I am currently the trustee of several charities including BBC Children in Need, where I am the youngest on the board. I have spoken passionately on TV and radio and in newspapers about social issues, and worked on a number of high-profile campaigns: from encouraging people to vote on election day, to addressing significant issues around the criminal justice system and social mobility. Through this work, I secured a place in the *Forbes* 30 Under 30 list for social impact.

My desire to make money and lift myself out of

poverty has never gone away, but these days it's legitimate. My proudest venture to date is Clear-View Research, which I co-founded with Burphy Zumu and Leonie Bellio. Through it, we give people from minority and under-represented backgrounds a voice in research, while working with organizations who give a damn about inclusion and diversity. With the support of a phenomenal team, it has grown to a seven-figure business. Now, we are providing bursaries to students from the same kinds of backgrounds as myself – investing in their futures and the futures of their communities.

I have wanted to give back in other ways, too. Through charity work I've supported young people into apprenticeships and employment who would otherwise be excluded from the jobs market. I have mentored dozens of people – providing the love and support they need to become the best versions of themselves, as well as challenging them along the way. Some of these people are men serving long-term prison sentences. Another project I am currently leading on is a community called Character Builders, which brings together around a hundred members of the Black community to build our characters – the most essential part of leadership. Can you believe that this 29-year-old Kenny was that foolish and reckless teenager shottin weed?

Back then, I had no idea that boy could grow up to be the person I am today. I saw value in money and status. I always thought that being in touch with my emotions was a weakness. I was more concerned with how people perceived me, rather than who I truly was. I learned the hard way to be the person I truly am – but my co-defendants are still living a nightmare. Sodiq and David remain in prison as both of their appeals against their convictions were denied. Their fight continues. I still visit them and support them, and will continue to do so. Their story could so easily have been mine.

Around me street life continues. Peckham has changed but it's still the hood. And when its deprived population are moved elsewhere and more affluent people move in, then Peckham's problems leapfrog to another area. These are the same problems of poverty and disillusionment, poor aspiration and poor resources. By the time this book is published, many of the statistics may be out of date. The Covid-19 pandemic, and now an economic crisis, will likely see educational and policing budgets cut, perhaps even benefits.

I cannot stand by and watch this happen. I do not want people from communities like mine to be cast out further than they already are. I have to keep fighting to give others a chance at a life only the privileged few can easily grab. I may not have made it to be Prime Minister (yet!), but I work every day to make a difference. Since The Kenny Report, I have written two more. The third was launched in 2015 and was the biggest youth-led report in the UK at the time, with twenty-four young authors contributing to it.

My journey started with determination, but I've also learned that it progresses with forgiveness. At the time of writing, my dad and I have a better relationship. I have forgiven him and shown him grace, which is all that we deserve. I have also got better at forgiving myself and this has enabled me to show love to others. I have hung up my 'player' boots and grown up. I am soon to be married to the beautiful Chantel-Marieé Jade Lewis – she doesn't know yet what she has said yes to!

Most of all, I look to those younger than me to keep me feeling positive and strong for the future, knowing that we need to catch children before they fall into the same cycles of poverty and violence. As we know, it is easier to build strong children than to repair broken men. Sodiq's daughter is now thirteen years old, and she is growing gracefully by the day. We regularly spend time together and the last time I saw her we played virtual reality games. Admittedly, some of the old Kenny still remains: I did not let her win and I am not ashamed to say it either.

I still live in Peckham and I love the place. It's my home, and it's where my heart is at. The experiences I have had growing up; everything that has, or has not, happened to me while living here has made me the man I am today. Prior to its gentrification, Peckham had such a bad reputation for what a very small minority did, and not the majority. Lots of talented and capable people who have come out of Peckham are seeing their dreams become a reality. If that can happen here, it can happen anywhere. Now, I couldn't be more proud to be *That Peckham Boy.*

Acknowledgements

Firstly and most importantly, I would like to give my ultimate thanks to God for everything He has done, is doing, and is yet to do in my life. If it were not for His grace, favour and unfailing love, I would never be where I am today.

My eternal gratitude also goes to my beautiful and selfless mother who has made countless sacrifices to give me and my younger brother George the best possible start in life. The stupid and poor decisions I made growing up are in no way a reflection of your parenting, just a result of my own childish, selfish, and arrogant ways. Thank you for pushing me when I was younger to know God and His word, even when I couldn't have been less interested. The older I get, the more appreciation I have for you. You have endured so much heartache because of me, and I am truly glad that now I am able to make you proud and give you more than a hundred reasons to smile. To my stepdad David

Afolabi, thank you for loving Mum, and for loving me and George like your own two sons. Thank you for showing up every week for me when I was in prison and at my darkest hour. To my brother George Imafidon, thank you for being the inspiration you are today, and for learning from my mistakes. Who would have ever thought that from fixing bikes when you were younger, I would now be witnessing you winning the Young Engineer of the Year award at the Royal Academy of Engineering? I was excited about winning just one scholarship to go to university, but you secured six. You keep raising the bar higher. To say I am proud of you would be an understatement.

Thanks also go to Kemi 'MVP' Ogunsanwo, my amazing literary agent, who believed in the vision for this book. I couldn't have picked anyone better to represent me; my editor at Transworld, Kate Fox, and Helena Drakakis, for your constructive feedback and magic touch. I have become a better writer through learning from you both; my no-nonsense aunty and agent for the last decade, Dr Diahanne Rhiney. Thank you for looking out for my best interests, and for your advice and encouragement; to Jonathon Toy, thank you for believing in me and supporting me and my family during our highs and lows. Your backing of The Kenny Report in 2012 was pivotal to shaping my career; thanks also to my mentor and third dad (yes, I am lucky enough to have three), Lord Michael Hastings, for supporting me and challenging me. You have loved me like a son, and I am indebted to you. You have opened my eyes to so much, and now I can't fly in economy class any more because of you. You've introduced me to businesspeople and leaders across the world, and brought me into rooms and spaces I would never ever have been invited into. Thanks also for your commitment to My Brother's Keeper, the organization we co-founded. You've faithfully joined me on thirty-six prison visits so far, and we've both had the pleasure of mentoring hundreds of men; to my business partner Burphy Zumu, thank you for sticking with me all the way, I couldn't have done it all without you. Both you and the one and only Leke Anthony have spent hours reading through various drafts and providing honest and brutal feedback; John Apena, my brother from another mother, thank you for walking this journey of life closely with me, and for your trustworthiness and loyalty starting in our teenage years; to Sodiq Adeojo and David Nyamupfukudza, it has been twelve years now that you have both been inside. The strength and positive outlook you both continue to show despite your circumstances, keeps me going at my lowest moments. It goes without saying I will never give up on you; and thanks to my soon-to-be-wife

Chantel-Marieé Jade Lewis for your moral support and for being my number one cheerleader. I love you always and can't wait to go on this lifetime adventure with you.

I also have to big up myself and all the other authors out there. I can't lie. I totally underestimated the time, energy and work that comes with writing a book, which has taken me five years. The process has been testing, but it brings me joy to now share it with you all.

Notes

1: Daddy Issues

1 https://www.ons.gov.uk/peoplepopulationandcom munity/birthsdeathsandmarriages/families/bulletins/ familiesandhouseholds/2019#london-had-the-highest-proportion-of-lone-parent-families-in-the-uk-in-2019

2 https://www.centreforsocialjustice.org.uk/wp-content/ uploads/2017/11/The-forgotten-role-of-families-why-its-time-to-find-our-voice-on-families-1.pdf

3 https://www.ncbi.nlm.nih.gov/pmc/articles/PMC 3904543/

4 S. Erath and K. Bierman (2006), 'Aggressive marital conflict, maternal harsh punishment, and child aggressive-disrupted behavior: evidence for direct and mediated relations', *Journal of Family Psychology*, 20(2): pp. 217–226

5 https://www.ncbi.nlm.nih.gov/pmc/articles/PMC 3904543/

2: My Brother's Keeper

1 https://www.ons.gov.uk/peoplepopulationandcommu
nity/healthandsocialcare/healthandlifeexpectancies/
articles/lifeexpectancycalculator/2019-06-07

5: You Could Become Prime Minister One Day

1 https://li.com/news/research-showing-impact-of-
universal-credit-cut-840000-more-people-in-poverty/

7: Looking at a Thirty-Year Sentence

1 https://www.ucl.ac.uk/news/2020/dec/londons-most-
deprived-neighbourhoods-see-more-stop-and-searches
2 Ibid.

8: Prison Break

1 https://prisonreformtrust.org.uk/wp-content/uploads/
2022/07/Prison-the-facts-2022.pdf
2 https://www.parliament.uk/business/publications/
written-questions-answers-statements/written-question/
Commons/2018-05-15/144303/
3 Ministry of Justice (2019), *Economic and social costs of reoffend-ing*, London: Ministry of Justice
4 https://ifs.org.uk/taxlab/key-questions/what-does-
government-spend-money
5 Tables 2.5a and 2.5b, Ministry of Justice (2020), 'Offender management statistics quarterly: April to June 2020', London: Ministry of Justice

6 https://www.gov.uk/government/publications/prison-
   education-a-review-of-reading-education-in-prisons/
   prison-education-a-review-of-reading-education-in-
   prisons#fnref:13

7 https://assets.publishing.service.gov.uk/government/
   uploads/system/uploads/attachment_data/file/278837/
   prisoners-childhood-family-backgrounds.pdf

11: Ashamed of My Own Name

1 https://prisonreformtrust.org.uk/wp-content/uploads/
   2022/07/Prison-the-facts-2022.pdf

2 https://prisonreformtrust.org.uk/wp-content/uploads/
   2022/07/Prison-the-facts-2022.pdf

3 Ibid.

12: It Pays to Be Yourself

1 https://assets.publishing.service.gov.uk/government/
   uploads/system/uploads/attachment_data/file/1098232/
   psi-72-2011-discharge.pdf

2 https://www.gov.uk/government/publications/unlock-
   opportunity-employer-information-pack-and-case-
   studies/employing-prisoners-and-ex-offenders

About the Author

Kenny Imafidon is a social entrepreneur, political commentator and activist. He is the co-founder and managing director of ClearView Research, which specializes in research and engagement projects focused on diverse and under-represented communities. Kenny has written influential and award-winning publications and has led innovative partnerships with global brands such as Uber, Tinder and Deliveroo on campaigns to get young people registered to vote and to turn out in elections. Kenny is a trustee of several charities, including BBC Children in Need. In 2022 he was featured in Forbes' annual 30 Under 30 list for social impact.